Expensive *Christian* Experiences

Viewing the Word of God Through Practical Living

Kefira Reid

Light
PUBLISHERS

ISBN: 978-1-953759-12-2

Acknowledgments

I must express gratitude to the sovereign God who has sustained me during the process of writing this devotional.

I would like to thank my husband, Mario Reid, for his moral support and for believing in my abilities.

Thanks to my publisher, Crystal S. Daye, who journeyed with me and facilitated me in the publishing of this devotional.

I am truly appreciative and grateful for all the support and prayers I have received. I am truly blessed and thankful: prayer changed my situation and made this book a reality.

Table of Contents

Introduction

It is costly to follow Jesus. It will cost us some things for us to be His disciples. It will cost us heartbreak, hurts, disappointments, discouragement, and, sometimes, physical pain. Yet, in all these things, He has been there for us.

Isaiah 43:2 says, *"When you pass through the waters, I will be with you; and when you pass through the rivers, they will not sweep over you. When you walk through the fire, you will not be burned; the flames will not set you ablaze."*

The Cost of Discipleship

Luke 9:56-62 has made it clear that following Jesus is costly. Scenarios from the verses give a clear understanding of this. One of the men said to Jesus that he wanted to follow Him. Jesus responded that He had no place to live. Jesus then said to another, "Come follow Me," but he replied that he wanted to go and bury his father first. Jesus said to him, "Let the dead bury their dead," but you must go and preach the kingdom for God. Another wanted to follow Jesus but wanted to say goodbye to his family first. Jesus ended by saying no one who puts his hand to the plough and looks back is fit for the kingdom of God.

I did not give up much to follow Jesus. I was a child when I surrendered my life to Him: twelve years old, to be exact. But as I grew in Christ, and Christ grew in me, I encountered life-changing experiences that broke me and strengthened me. I encountered failures and victories, brokenness, resentment, and loneliness. I also gave my share of unpleasantness on the Christian pathway. There were times when I was the one who had struggles dealing with and took it out on others, and they were frustrated with me as well.

In all these experiences, God has always been there. I have learned that He has His hands on me. Even the times when I walked away, He always chastens me, even when it hurts.

Hebrews 12:6-11
Because the Lord disciplines the one he loves, and he chastens
everyone he accepts as his son. Endure hardship as discipline;
God is treating you as his children. For what children are not
disciplined by their father? If you are not disciplined—and
everyone undergoes discipline—then you are not legitimate,
not true sons and daughters at all. Moreover, we have all had
human fathers who disciplined us and we respected them for
it. How much more should we submit to the Father of spirits
and live! They disciplined us for a little while as they thought
best; but God disciplines us for our good, in order that we may
share in his holiness. No discipline seems pleasant at the time,
but painful. Later on, however, it produces a harvest of
righteousness and peace for those who have been trained by it.

These Christian experiences are not only common to many
persons but are expensive as I sacrificed a lot to reach this stage
in my Christian journey. The journey is not yet complete, but I
saddle up for the experiences to come and wait for them to
unfold.

Day 1
Procrastination

What is procrastination? Procrastination is the action of delaying or postponing something. Jim Howard wrote: "Whatever form your procrastination comes in, learn to identify it, root and kick it out!"

Ecclesiastes 9:10
Whatever your hand finds to do, do it with all your might, for in the realm of the dead, where you are going, there is neither working nor planning nor knowledge nor wisdom.

Procrastinating is something I have been doing for a long time. It took a whole lot for me to put myself out there. Truth is, no matter how good I am, someone will see the bad; no matter how authentic I am, some will see me as fake; no matter how I hide from the world, I will still be affected by things that happen in the world because I temporarily live here.

We cannot have life-changing experiences boxed up in the four walls of our homes and minds. It is more terrifying to be locked up in the mind than anything else. But when we are transformed by the renewing of our minds (See Romans 12:2), then great things happen. We can have a colorful canvas, each color telling a different life story of hope.

Day 2
Surpassing People's Expectations

I was labeled "most likely to fail in everything I did" at one point while growing up. They got that impression because I gave them something to work with. As I grew in the Lord, and the Lord grew in me, He refined me and continues to grow in me through His Word. He encouraged me with a word from Proverbs 12:18. He said that I have a future, and my hope will not be cut off. I may have taken a long time to let the Word sink in because of how messed up I was, but the Lord kept shattering their expectations.

There are some who still have reservations about me failing and failing miserably, but my Father, my Sustainer, my Keeper; the Good Shepherd who never leaves His sheep to be lost and lonely, told me I will never fail, even if I fall. He is a promise-keeping God. His Word states in Proverbs 10:28: "The prospect of the righteous is joy, but the hopes of the wicked come to nothing." Therefore, I will not fail.

Develop a habit of surpassing people's expectations, good or bad.

~ Kefira Reid

Day 3
Dream Big

Proverbs 3:5-6
Trust in the Lord with all your heart and lean not on your own
understanding; in all your ways submit to him, and he will
make your paths straight.

I have repeated this scripture many times, and it sometimes seems hard to believe. But scripture tells me that unbelief is a sin, so what do I do? If I am ever going to get any results from God, then I must exercise my faith in Him by trusting His Word, even when others see otherwise.

Whose report on your life will you believe? If God has shown it to you, then it will come to pass. It is not just a figment of your imagination. While you were busy with other things, He was taking you through a process and preparing you for what is to come. Though you saw it as just a gift, God saw it as an instrument to carry out His mandate. If you can perceive it, you will achieve it. The foundation is being laid, and soon the blueprint will become a reality.

Day 4
Christian's Breast Milk

At thirteen-months old, my daughter was still breastfeeding in between meals and snacks. She wanted it when she was sleepy, fussy, and happy.

Breast milk provides the ideal nutrition for infants, and it is provided in a form more easily digested than infant formula. Breast milk contains antibodies that help babies to fight off viruses and bacteria. Breastfeeding lowers a baby's risk of having asthma or allergies.

My baby is healthy and strong and has a clean skin and a fluffy body I am not tired of looking at. This is so because she has, and is, taking in the right combination of foods, especially breast milk.

At some point, my milk supply will run out, but she would have received everything she needs to aid her in growing healthy and would have performed the basic preventative measures against certain diseases.

1 Peter 2:2-3
Like newborn babies, crave pure spiritual milk, so that by it you may grow up in your salvation, now that you have tasted that the Lord is good.

There were moments in my life I was craving everything else but the Word of God. Those things only brought me temporary relief and left a huge emptiness inside. When my back was against the wall, and I needed answers, I had to go where God spoke, and that was in His Word.

I have grown and am still growing, and it is beautiful. I am not perfect, but I see where habits are breaking, and new habits are forming. God be praised!

As Christians, we have breast milk: THE WORD OF GOD. It does not just lower the risk of sinning; it can totally eradicate sin if our intake is enough and duly digested. We can intake this milk when we are feeling low, sad, happy, frustrated, and indecisive.

Along with this breast milk, we have other combinations of nutritional foods, such as prayer, love, forgiveness, fasting, worship, and fellowship. When all these are digested, we become healthy and strong, with a clean inside that reflects on our outside, and people will be attracted to us. The supply of milk, the Word of God, is always there. It can never run out or go dry. It is highly recommended to take in the morning, afternoon, evenings, in between meals and just whenever because it is readily available for our consumption.

Day 5
Five Christian Vitamin Cs

I bought a plate of pineapple, took the first bite, and my entire facial expression changed when my taste buds connected to the tingling sourness. I turned to my husband with one eye closed and said, "No sah, dis cut nature."

His reply, "No, it's vitamin C."

You may have tasted, or are about to taste, something sour in your life; it is not meant to kill you or cut you off, but it is vitamin C. It will repair the brokenness you have come to experience. That vitamin C is for COURAGE; courage to CONTINUE the path you think is unbearable. At the end, you will be strengthened and healthy.

You squeeze your face now because of the taste your CIRCUMSTANCES left on you, but it will make you stronger.

You squeeze your face, but you are exercising CONTROL over the situation. Persevere in your sourness because endurance produces CHARACTER, and CHARACTER produces hope. Take your vitamin Cs!

COURAGE: Strength amid pain.

CONTINUE: Persist in an activity or process.

CIRCUMSTANCES: A fact or condition connected with or relevant to an event or action.

CONTROL: Determine the behavior or supervise the running of.

Day 6
Accepting God's Answer

I was conflicted about a matter, so I spoke to the Lord about it, and He gave me an answer. Upon hearing the noise from people around me; hearing of other people's experiences, and the possibility of the same happening to me, I began to question the answer I received from God. I went ahead to prove if the answer from God was right or it was just my mind. I was exposed by the Lord for my lack of trust and belief in Him.

Have you ever been shamed by God? Many times, I have reduced His Word from what it is by not trusting and believing what He says. Even as I write, I still have the feeling I had when I doubted God. It is a lingering feeling of disappointment in myself. How could I have doubted God when He has spoken to me so many times and given me answers to queries so many times? Even with all these disappointments within myself, He still shows me love.

In my bed, He speaks to my subconscious and says: "It's not for Me to force you to believe. You must willingly trust and believe."

When God gives you an answer on a matter, do not doubt Him. The Bible says: "My sheep knows My voice and they follow me" (See John 10:27-28). Do not get distracted by the noise around you. Even if all indications surrounding the matter seem to go in the direction of the noise, and it seems like they are right, do not detour from the answer God has given you. God has never lied and can never lie. If you go ahead and try to prove your answer, you are still going to end up being WRONG because God's Word is "Yes and AMEN."

Day 7
Change Requires Work

William McDowell's song of intercession has a stanza that says: *"The change I want to see must first begin with me. I surrender, so your world can be changed."*

I raised my hands to comb my hair, and I glanced at my hands. I did not like what I saw; they were fatter than I would want them to be. On top of that, I had clothing in my closet that I loved, but the hands were not fitting. I decided, "Oh no, I cannot carry on like this. I need to do something about it." So, I started my workout with stones to help me lose the desired weight on the hands.

It burns, and my hands were sore. I felt the fat burning. In the days, I felt like my hands were useless. I thought of not continuing and just work with what I have, but every time I looked in the mirror, I saw my hands. So, I continued and will continue. My neighbor saw me and asked if I was working on my summer body.

If you look in the mirror and you do not like what you see, change it. Wherever you are in your life right now, whether spiritually, physically, emotionally, financially or socially, it is your decision to make: you can either stay where you are or get up and do something about it. When you make a move, things are going to get rough. It will burn; you will feel like quitting but do not quit. People will have things to say when they see you getting up and start doing something to change your status. They will say, for example, "What are you trying to play?" if it relates to your spiritual life. "Are you trying to be Oprah?" if it relates to your financial status. "You want to be the next top model!" if it relates to your physical appearance. They will want to know if you have upgraded if it relates to your emotional stability.

Do not mind the noise; use it as a motivation to get where you need to be.

DO THE WORKOUT!

Day 8
No Results In Worrying

Philippians 4:6-7
Do not be anxious about anything, but in every situation, by prayer and petition, with thanksgiving, present your requests to God. And the peace of God, which transcends all understanding, will guard your hearts and your minds in Christ Jesus.

Over the years, I have heard this scripture, read this scripture, but failed to apply this scripture. I worry about things that it affected me both emotionally and physically, and what has it changed? Nothing! The answer did not come any faster, the money did not come any quicker, and the confusion did not get any clearer.

I finally caught up with the schemes of the devil, and he has no new tricks. He recycles his strategies and re-launches them, and because we are so caught up in our emotional trauma, we overlook the fact that it is the same fight with different scenarios. I have learned, and continue to learn, the ways of God, so I can overcome any obstacle the enemy throws at me. I am now reaping the results of trusting God and His plans and directives for my life. I am resting in His hands, knowing He is more than capable of handling everything concerning me.

Day 9
Feeding The Spirit

I had a mango and some juice. My system got weak, and each time I got up to get something done, I just dropped right back on the chair. On top of that, I was breastfeeding throughout the night.

John 6:35
Then Jesus declared, "I am the bread of life. Whoever comes to me will never go hungry, and whoever believes in me will never be thirsty."

Most people eat bread, whether it be whole-wheat or white bread. We have it for breakfast; we can have it for lunch, and we can also have it for dinner. In the same way we consume the physical bread, we must likewise eat the bread of life, which is the Word of God. If we do not feed the spirit man, he will become dormant and eventually die.

We cannot keep giving out and not taking in anything, or we are going to shut down, unable to move towards anything concerning God or people. When we eat this bread, it gives us the strength for the journey ahead. We already do not have enough laborers for the harvest, so we cannot afford to be stagnant. In the same way our bodies need food to function, so too our spirit needs spiritual food to function. The Word of God has everything nutritious for the spirit and body and for every aspect of life.

Day 10
Where Our Treasures Lie

I was sitting by my favorite spot one morning, and while I was there reflecting on the goodness of God in my life, thanking Him for keeping me thus far, my mind drifted a little. I wondered if those who were established, both in and out of the church (I say "in church" because there are people who are Christians, but have not given themselves to sacred worship to God), have been privileged to enjoy some form of materialistic substance. Are they asking what impact exuberant worship to God and commitment to ministry when it comes on to church has done for you? I wondered what comparisons they were making with themselves and me; are they saying, "I have not done all that, but look at what I have accomplished or gained?"

I was so consumed with the thought that I left a bedspread unpinned on the cloths-line, just to direct my thoughts to hubby. He said, "My answer to them would be, I am not working to store up treasures on earth, but to have treasures in heaven." What I do for God is not to get an earthly reward. He knows what our needs are, and even though He said ask, I will not reduce my enthusiasm and exuberance in worship just because I am not getting the materialistic provisions I asked for.

Do we do what we do to get earthly rewards? Why should we not be exuberant in our worship of God? After all, He paid the ultimate sacrifice of dying a death we could not. He continues to make intercessions on our behalf because of the rebelliousness of our hearts. Why go after the world's treasures, gaining the houses, cars, money, and you name it, when our souls are not secured in the most treasured place with God?

Whatever thought your mind generates that seem to undermine the things you do for God, questioning whether or not what you do is worth not having what others seem to be enjoying, ensure you have a counteracting, evidential answer to erase it. The devil will point out what you are not getting and what is not happening for you in an attempt to cut your enthusiasm so you fall back into mediocrity in your worship and giving, inclusive of your time and substance. Remember, the Bible says:

Matthew 6:19-21
Do not store up for yourselves treasures on earth, where moths and vermin destroy, and where thieves break in and steal. But store up for yourselves treasures in heaven, where moths and vermin do not destroy, and where thieves do not break in and steal. For where your treasure is, there your heart will be also.

Day 11
Don't Quit!

Recently I found a quote by Lance Armstrong that says: "The struggle is temporary, quitting is forever."
I have thought of quitting many times. In fact, I quit so many things in my mind; some of them I did literally, but to this day, the decision to quit has had serious repercussions on me. The moment I encounter a struggle, sometimes my first solution is to quit: quit the church, quit school, quit my marriage. Thank God for the power of the Spirit who lives in me.

Sometimes quitting seems to be the only option when faced with a difficult situation. I should not have, I am sorry I did, why did I, are words we use in these difficult moments. God's Spirit aids us in our weaknesses.

Isaiah 40:29-31 states: "He gives strength to the weary and increases the power of the weak. Even youths grow tired and weary, and young men stumble and fall; but those who hope in the Lord will renew their strength. They will soar on wings like eagles; they will run and not grow weary; they will walk and not be faint."

Do not quit!
#activatingthewarriorinme

Day 12
Am I Ready For A Deeper Experience In God?

Exodus 33:18-23

Then Moses said, "Now show me your glory." And the Lord said, "I will cause all my goodness to pass in front of you, and I will proclaim my name, the Lord, in your presence. I will have mercy on whom I will have mercy, and I will have compassion on whom I will have compassion. But," he said, "you cannot see my face, for no one may see me and live." Then the Lord said, "There is a place near me where you may stand on a rock. When my glory passes by, I will put you in a cleft in the rock and cover you with my hand until I have passed by. Then I will remove my hand and you will see my back; but my face must not be seen."

I think I am ready for a deeper experience with God, but am I really? Having a deeper experience in God comes with added responsibilities and added troubles. Am I ready to have guns being pointed in my face? Am I ready for people to threaten me with witchcraft and threats of violence in the name of warfare?

It is all good when I am in the four walls of the church, and other people see me as a warrior, doing the things they think a warrior would do, but having no real combat with the enemy.

30

How would I react if I were backed up at church and given an ultimatum to continue or not continue pursuing Christ? It is good to quote scriptures like Paul, saying I am crucified with Christ, and I bear the mark of Jesus Christ in my body, but will I do like Peter and deny Him for the sake of saving my life? Yes, Paul says to live is Christ and to die is gain, but am I Paul? So, do I not fear for my life? I would love the opportunity to live a fulfilled life; I would love to live to see my children all grown up and see how they turn out. Do I want to be involved in people's spiritual battles that will unleash backlash from the enemy, putting my family in danger? I love God, but loving God comes with all these and more.

Do I still want a deeper experience with God? YES, yes, I do. These deeper experiences not only prove the God I serve, but it takes me to a place of total surrender. It activates the will to trust Him, regardless of how bad I think a situation is. It allows me to walk in confidence knowing that not one tittle of His word passes because He would have fulfilled every promise He made concerning those who trust Him.

A deeper experience with God allows me to know Him and the power of His resurrection, which anchors me deeply in Him. Deeper experiences bring to life the scripture: "My grace is sufficient to keep you and my grace is made perfect in your weakness" (See 2 Corinthians 12:9).

Finally, I need deeper experiences with God because my experiences are not for my own documentation; it is to help others to come into a deeper relationship with Jesus Christ and to proudly model the character of Christ through what I go through.

Day 13
He's An Intentional God

I was thinking about life and all the changes that happened and continues to happen in my life. Some have more effect than others. Some still have me in suspense.

While I may be a primary contributor to many, there are some happenings that I just do not know how they came about. I could sit all day and try to iron out why things happen the way they do, and I could say it is the enemy or say it is God bringing me through a phase. Whatever the case may be, it is happening. Maybe I will not get an answer; not yet anyway.

As I reached towards my cupboard, I heard the words of a song by Travis Greene in my head: "All things are working for my good; He's intentional, never failing."

#activation #contentment #iserveanintentionalGod

It is easy to say, "Do not worry about it," but we struggle not to worry; it is the natural human side of us to worry. As I encourage you, I encourage myself: do not worry; we serve an intentional God.

Jeremiah 1:5
Before I formed you in the womb, I knew you, before you were born I set you apart; I appointed you as a prophet to the nations.

You may not be a prophet, but whatever you are, or destined to be, He already knows.

Day 14
Broken But Valuable

Terri Gibbs penned the song: "He didn't throw the clay away."

The lyrics:

> Empty and broken, I came back to Him
> A vessel unworthy, so scarred with sin.
> But He did not despair, He started over again
> And I bless the day, He didn't throw the clay away.
>
> Over and over, He molds me and makes me,
> Into His likeness, He fashions the clay.
> A vessel of honor, I am today,
> All because Jesus didn't throw the clay away.
>
> He is the Potter, I am the clay
> And molded in His image, He wants me to stay.
> Oh, but when I stumble,
> When I fall,
> When my vessel breaks,
> He just picks up those pieces,
> He does not throw the clay away.

Even if you had an idea of how broken I was, I am the only one who can truly paint a picture of the broken state I was in. What

I thought was waste, He saw as golden. Though everything went into the disposal, He went searching through my trash for something useful. Who does that?

Even when I break, He chisels me into shape again. Did you think your trash was useless? God does not think like us. His ways are higher than our ways; His thoughts higher than our thoughts (See Isaiah 55:8-9), and His work is perfect.

#iserveanunconventionalartisticalkindaGod

Day 15
Activating My Will

Galatians 5:13
You, my brothers, and sisters, were called to be free. But do not use your freedom to indulge the flesh; rather, serve one another humbly in love.

I realize that some days my mood is just under the weather. I feel sad and linger in a state of depression. At times, I am not sure what causes me to feel and be that way. Maybe thoughts from my unconscious have resurfaced and dampened my mood. When that mood surfaces, the flesh is gratified, and the people around me are affected.

Whatever the cause may be, it is not a healthy place to be, so whenever that happens, I willfully change my mood, putting myself at a place of contentment by drawing from other things that are more pleasant.

God remains the same, but His methods of doing things are infinite. Because He is infinite, He has made provisions for us to live in His infinity.

The enemy is a copycat, and he remains the same. He comes to kill, steal, and destroy (See John 10:10) with the same strategies: depression, hopelessness, loneliness, violence, murders, and everything anti-God. His end is eternal damnation.

Now that you know where those feelings lie, let us make the switch and willfully decide not to stay within that state anymore.

Day 16
Be Fierce and Strong As You Roar

I saw a clip of a woman dressed in black, beating down another woman's door. She looked the part of a champion; looked well trained, she talked the talk and dressed the part. She paced back and forth, calling on her opponent to come out with a lot of noise. The lady inside pulled her door open and immediately sprang on the other woman. To my disappointment, she got her ass whooped badly.

I grew up hearing that empty barrels make the most noise. What sounds are you making? Can your sound be put to the test? We say we are warriors in the Lord; we talk like a warrior, carry weapons like a warrior, but can we fight like warriors? When demons and devils come upon us, attacking us, trying to defeat us, can we demonstrate what we were pacing back and forth for, dressed for, and roared for?

If we are going to proceed to the enemy's camp, please ensure that you do not only roar. The devil also roars, but he is not a lion. We are empowered by the conquering Lion of the tribe of Judah, who lives in us and gives us the fighting skills a lion possesses.

A lion does not only make loud noises, but its attack is also fierce and strong. Is your noise a reflection of the strength you carry?

#sound #strength #battle #win

DAY 17
Don't Sit In Your Mess

My second son, Eljoenai, was about to have a bath to go to school one morning, but, as usual, baby Hannah went into the bathroom with Dad so she could see her brother take a bath. She pooped, and I was about to clean her up, but as she saw her brother taking off his clothes to enter the bathroom, she sat down at the door and would not move. All the pretty names and sweet baby talks could not move her to come and get cleaned up, as she wanted to go into the bathroom. I picked her up. I took her diaper off; the mess was plastered all over because she sat in it, so it went to places it should not have been.

Mess is a dirty, untidy state of things or a place. Mess is a situation that is confusing and filled with problems. A messy situation leads to depression, hopelessness, and lack of concentration. A messy mind is a clogged mind that interferes with the ability to think and make wise decisions.

Are you sitting down in a messy situation, refusing to get up because of the anticipation of engaging in something that is not beneficial to you? Are you refusing to get up and answer the call to be cleaned because you enjoy the pleasure of what you see over on the other side? Are you slipping out of God's hand when He picks you up to get you cleaned up, wriggling and crying to go back to situations that are not good for you? Well, stop! Look at what the mess has done to you. Your refusal to get up and be cleaned results in the mess going into places in your life it should not have. Your whole life is chaotic because of this mess; people are being affected by you sitting in your mess because you spread it on people it should not have been on.

You need to get rid of that mess that is detrimental to your health and stop focusing on what or who is in the other room. You are confused and filled with problems because you are sitting down in a mess. You lack concentration because you are sitting down in a mess. The person in the other room is focusing on being cleaned, and that is why they are undressing. Look at the mess you are in and focus on getting cleaned as well. As a matter of fact, your Father is calling you. Do not let Him have to snatch you up. Get up and go!

Day 18
Faith Through My Struggles

Whatever questions we may have about God's existence through what we experience in our personal lives, does not take away from the fact that He is there.

Our struggles may indicate that He is not present, and He does not make sense, but maybe He allows us to go through struggles to show us He is there.

I remember going to Kenilworth Academy. It was a struggle for me to travel because it was rough financially. One week, I had to be fighting to find the fare to go back and forth. I had no fare one evening, and one of my classmates offered to pay my way to the park. To get home from there was the other big problem as I was not familiar with the taxis on the route. I walked and looked down on the ground, hoping to find some coins to help. I went from Bay West to Sam Sharpe Square but did not find a dollar. I began to cry, and I turned my eyes towards heaven. I said, "God, I have been serving You from I was twelve years old. Have You brought me this far to embarrass me?" I mentioned to Him that I had gotten many opportunities to be immoral, but I remained true to Him because I love Him. I then repeated His Word to Him in Matthew 6:35-27. I was anxious because I did not know how I was going to reach home. I said, "Didn't You promise to take care of me like the birds in air? Am I not more valuable than they?" I cried and spoke to Him. Suddenly, my cousin drove up, and I got a free ride home.

As much as we want to be in control and want everything to make sense, it is not for us to make sense of it. He has everything under control, though we may not see it that way. Our state of being is being bombarded with the pressures of life, and we want quick fixes, but these quickies do not always work.

Struggles present, struggles absent, being in and out of control is not a factor of His existence; be convinced that He exist: that is called FAITH.

Day 19
Going Through The Fire

I decided one Saturday that the family would enjoy some baked breadfruit for breakfast. I prepared the breadfruit for the oven and left it there to be completed. Little did I know that the gas was low, and before the breadfruit was finished, the gas ran out. It was half baked, so I decided to put it on some wood fire. My husband came and made the fire, and I roasted it.

After preparing it, and we started eating, I could not believe that it was the same yellow-heart breadfruit. It was dry and hard to swallow; we could not eat much because it was too dry.

When we are on fire for God, and we are being baked in His goodness and mercies and processed for coronation, and our fire goes out halfway there, do not resort to other alternatives. Do not go to roasting when God has already decided to bake you. We cannot start on a pathway that is smooth inside and outside and then resort to a path where the outside is black and the inside dry. When we become black and dry, no one will be able to digest us. Let us contact the gas man (JESUS) to refuel our fire so we can come out as He intended for us to be, so those who come across our path, or to whoever path we cross, will experience God's goodness through us.

Jesus is the thermometer for our fire. His Word tells us in Isaiah 43:2, *"When you pass through the waters, I will be with you; and when you pass through the rivers, they will not sweep over you. When you walk through the fire, you will not be burned; the flames will not set you ablaze."*

The flames will not set you ablaze because He is managing the temperature of the fires we are in.

Day 20
My Forever Friend

Throughout my existence, I have had many friendships. Many sprang up conditionally and died quickly. Many turned away from me when they got to know the real me. I was not up for mediocrity in my Christian life or any other aspect of my life. For some, I was not popular enough; for others, I could not spoil them with the material things they desired from a friend.

With Jesus, I am not in a relationship that is based on conditions. He loved me first, so I have no choice but to love Him in return. He knew me, knew what I would have done, knows what I will be doing in the future, yet He loves me with an everlasting love.

John 15:13
Greater love has no one than this: to lay down one's life for one's friends.

In this friendship, He loves me more than I love Him. He has never turned His back on me. He has never cheated on me. He has never judged me. He has always provided for me, always protected me from myself and from the enemy. His plans for me are to prosper me and to see me in good health.

In spite of all that is happening, I will be like Abraham: believe God so He can credit me with righteousness and remain in a friendship with Him.

#exclusivefriendship/relationship

Day 21
Failed Approach In Address To God

I was in awe in the shower one day when God said, "Things could have been different, but you stopped praying." I was thinking about a situation when He responded. This tore me up. I began to question Him. I know I used to have some formal prayers, writing prayers in my prayer journal, but what about the conversations under the tree, what about the shower talks, the little mumblings here and there, did that count for something? In my questioning, He said, "You were not praying; you were complaining. Prayer is communication, and you were not communicating; you were arguing."

Communication is a two-way street. I must also listen and not just talk. If I were listening, I would have heard His answers to many questions and the instructions given.

Things were not going to change, and the moment I heard the first statement, His confirmation came with His Word in James 4:3: *"When you ask, you do not receive, because you ask with wrong motives, that you may spend what you get on your pleasures."* He did not have a problem with my strategy; He had a problem with my approach.

One month later, I resumed proper communication. Everything I was concerned about was already completed.

Listen! If you are faced with any situation, and you are questioning the outcome, before you check God on it, check your contribution towards it. Have you been praying or complaining? Communicating or arguing? You see, God will allow us to argue our way, like Job, but when you are done, and He starts His line speech, you best believe you are going to be found guilty.

#dothereverse #stopcomplaing #startpraying #stoparguing #startcommunicating

Day 22
Let Your Light Shine

I am not sure if you can feel it, but the darkness is getting thicker and heavier than before. This darkness has taken over the church, and Christians are acting the fool. People are being wise in their own eyes; a great falling away has been taking place, and it may not get any better because Timothy wrote about it.

1 Timothy 4:1-2
The Spirit clearly says that in later times some will abandon the faith and follow deceiving spirits and things taught by demons. Such teachings come through hypocritical liars, whose consciences have been seared as with a hot iron.

The devil has deceived many and will continue to deceive many others. We must let the light that is within us (Jesus) shine so bright that the darkness cannot comprehend it. Now is not the time to point fingers or cast blame; now is the time to ensure that our lives are ready for the great day that is coming.

Jesus did not hide anything concerning following Him; our crosses are different, but the grace and the strength that He gives for the journey is the same. If you have been stumbling on your path, check to see if your light has been turned low. If it has, put more oil in the lamp and turn up the light. Add more oil of prayer, oil of being willful in your actions, oil of fellowship, oil of forgiveness, and the Word. Let Jesus shine bright and eliminate the darkness.

Day 23
God Of All Situations

The word "situation" is explained as a set of circumstances in which one finds oneself. Whether they were unavoidable or not, we are faced with them daily. Paul wrote in his epistle to the Romans:

Romans 8:28
And we know that in all things God works for the good of those who love him, who have been called according to his purpose.

When I sleep, there is a situation. When I awake, there is a situation. At church, there are situations; at home, there are situations. In the community where I reside, there are situations. When I drive, there are situations. Talking brings up situations, and if I do not talk, it becomes a situation.

Sometimes I have no solution to these situations, but whatever situation I find myself in, I am trusting that God knows the right situation to take me out of, the right situation for me to go through, and when to end a situation.

#trustingtheGodofsituations

Day 24
Choose Your Dirt Wisely

Genesis 2:7
Then the Lord God formed a man from the dust of the ground
and breathed into his nostrils the breath of life, and the man
became a living being.

James 1:21
Therefore, get rid of all moral filth and the evil that is so
prevalent and humbly accept the word planted in you, which
can save you.

Dirt is a mixture of a whole lot of stuff, including rocks, sand, clay, and organic matter. Another meaning for dirt is information about someone's activities or private life that could prove damaging if revealed.

We were all made from the dust of the earth. Scientifically, dirt is good and has many health benefits, but there is dirt that is bad; dirt that if it stays on us too long, can be damaging to us, literally. Then there is the dirt that damages reputations and smears a person. This kind of dirt makes you feel heavy, murky, and unclean.

I came home from a long day at church one day, and I was feeling hot and sweaty, sticky, and dirty. I felt so lousy and felt

54

sick, literally, because my body was dirty. Immediately, as I put some soap on my body, I felt the refreshing feeling coming on. As I rinsed the soap off, I began feeling even better.

You must know which dirt to let stay on you. If it is not the good dirt that will grow you, by feeding you with nutrients from its particles, then wash it off. Dirt is said to be good for your skin but know which dirt to let stick to you. You do not want to be sweaty, sticky, and lousy; that will make you sick and affect everyone else around you. You do not want to be giving off a foul odor because you have the wrong dirt on you.

Day 25
When God Responds

In my many years of existence and being a Christian, I have had many life-changing experiences. I have gone through many struggles and heart-breaking moments. I have had many pastors speaking into my life; they spoke prophesies and declarations; some I have seen and some yet to come to pass. To be honest, there are some I am still pondering.

In my lowest moments, when I feel all hope is lost, God uses the most unlikely people, situations, and places to affirm and re-affirm His love, and His hands on my life.

Jeremiah 29:12
Then you will call on me and come and pray to me, and I will listen to you.

While sitting in the afternoon session at a convention, our Caribbean Field Director was the speaker, and he brought the word from the Lord. He said God told him to tell His people that He has seen, heard, and has come down to help. He said, "You do not have to fight!" I was so tired and sleepy; literally, emotionally, and spiritually. I was not focused on anything or anybody. While sitting there, he asked us to raise our hands and receive the proclamation about God seeing, hearing, and helping. A lady, I will call her Lady J because I had never seen her before, stood and touched my husband and I on the shoulders, and said, "This is for both of you. No more tears, He's fighting for you." She left immediately. I looked to see where she went, but I could not see. I kept replaying the event in my head, and I asked my husband in the morning if he had seen where she went, and he said no.

Sometimes we are hoping that God would use the top preachers or highly recognizable people to speak to us, but God uses the most unlikely people to speak to us. The direction we are looking in is not where God is coming from. He always takes care of His own and in the right time. I thank God for His love concerning me, and though I may not see His plans for me now, I rest securely in His hands, knowing He is fighting for me.

Day 26
Victorious Loser

In this Christian journey, we are fighting a spiritual warfare against our fleshly desires. From time to time, we may experience failure, but do not worry, there are many examples of great men and women in the Bible who lost battles but ended victoriously. Paul encouraged us in 2 Corinthians 4:8-10: *We are hard pressed on every side, but not crushed; perplexed, but not in despair; persecuted, but not abandoned; struck down, but not destroyed. We always carry around in our body the death of Jesus, so that the life of Jesus may also be revealed in our body.*

We are no different than those we read about in the Bible. We may fail, but Jesus has already won the war against Satan when He conquered death, hell, and the grave and took the keys from his hands. You may have lost a battle but, remember, the weapons of our warfare are not carnal; they are mighty through God to the pulling down of strongholds(See 2 Corinthians 10:4-6). You lost, but you are a winner. We became winners when we were purchased by the resurrected Spirit of Jesus Christ. Because He rose victoriously, we automatically became victors by virtue of His status: King of kings and Lord of lords, conquering Lion of the tribe of Judah.

Day 27
Righteousness Over Recognition

Colossians 3:23-24
Whatever you do, work at it with all your heart, as working for the Lord, not for human masters, since you know that you will receive an inheritance from the Lord as a reward. It is the Lord Christ you are serving.

I was observing this text for a couple of days, and it plunged me into deep introspection of the work I do and every activity that I have been involved in. I was going over the different scenarios that I was a part of; the discussions, disagreements, relationships, just about everything that I was exposed to. At the end of all those introspections, my only prayer was to make everything I do count. To be an established writer is my most sought after desire, and I am doing everything legally possible to make it happen. Still, it would be sad if, after all this accomplishment, I find myself lost in eternity because I failed to practice what I speak or write about.

1 John 3:7
Dear children, do not let anyone deceive you about this: When people do what is right, it shows that they are righteous, even as Christ is righteous.

It rests on me heavily daily, and while prayer is good and necessary and is a great way to start, I must make the proper adjustments to ensure that I do not find myself before the judgment or in eternity regretting not taking a different path. It is good to keep hope alive and run with it, but I must put in the work in keeping faith alive.

Do not let the impressive work you do rob you of safeguarding your spot in glory; while pointing others to the way, you failed to follow the way yourself.

#righteousnessoverrecognition

Day 28
Be Humble While You Wait

---

1 Peter 5:6-7
Humble yourselves, therefore, under God's mighty hand, that
he may lift you up in due time. Cast all your anxiety on him
because he cares for you.

P eter was looked on as a caveman: dumb, but Peter had
an experience with Jesus that caused him to astonish
those he came across who had previously looked down
at him. Jesus declared that on Peter's confession, He would
build His church and the gates of hell will not prevail against
it. Today, Peter is a great example to whom we look, for he
experienced God for himself and wrote about it so we can have
his God-inspired Word as our guide.

Many years ago, I was one of those people looked down on. I
had gone through a rough period in my life, and persons
thought I would not amount to anything. When I was preparing
to get married, it was an issue. Going into ministry was an issue
for some because they saw me as unworthy and unqualified.
But God! Today, I am in a position that requires me to be the
example God has called me to be. Even though they saw me as
nothing before, God has elevated me so they can see His
goodness through me.

Do not worry if you are looked over and looked down on. Your failures and embarrassments will turn around for acknowledgment. You will have a turn around that causes people to look up to you as an example, and you will be used greatly by God to fulfill His mandate.

#whileiamwaiting

Day 29
Called Or Chosen

One morning I saw a practical example of the scripture that says the first will be last. I was washing my baby's clothes, and as I proceeded to get the bucket with her garments, I saw a pink onesie on top of the machine, took it up, and put in the bath with the already soapy water.

When I came back with the others, I put them in, pressing them down and stirring so the soap could reach every piece in the water. I turned them around, going under and up, then finally I started picking pieces to wash. It was not until the end of my washing that I realized the very same pink onesie that I had placed in the bath first was the last to be washed.

To my amazement, I chuckled, and scripture immediately sprung to the top of my thoughts.

Matthew 20:16
So, the last will be first, and the first will be last.

Many are called, but few chosen (See Matthew 22:14). Do not be so hasty to condemn or think of yourself as the "it." We may be among the "called," but our motives and actions determine whether we are chosen.

\#lineupyourmotiveandyouractionstomatchyourstatus
\#calledorchosen

Day 30
Focus On Your Own Test Paper

I can recall doing an accounting exam and reaching a particular question on the paper. I worked out the problem, got the answer, but happened to glance at my classmate's answer and doubted mine.

I asked her how she came by that answer, and even though I knew I had the correct formula, I changed it because there were others with the answer she had. When we got the paper back, it turned out that mine was right all along.

2 Timothy 2:15
Do your best to present yourself to God as one approved, a worker who does not need to be ashamed and who correctly handles the word of truth.

If you have studied, then you will be tested on what you have studied. Do not let the crowd's persuasion change your mind from the answer God has given you. The apostle Paul says in 2 Timothy 3:16-17: *"All Scripture is God-breathed and is useful for teaching, rebuking, correcting and training in righteousness, so that the servant of God may be thoroughly equipped for every good work."*

Go through with what you started with because looking over on another's test paper will warrant your failure.

#mytestmyanswer

Day 31
When Jesus Says No

A conversation is recorded in Luke 22:31-32 with Jesus and Peter: *"Simon, Simon, Satan has asked to sift all of you as wheat. But I have prayed for you, Simon, that your faith may not fail. And when you have turned back, strengthen your brothers."*

There is a song we often sing, which says, "When the devil say no, Jesus say yes," but have you experienced the devil saying yes, and Jesus says NO? The devil gets a lot of "NOs" from Jesus regarding my family and me:

- "No, you will not kill them."
- "No, you will not hurt them."
- "No, you will not separate them."
- "No, you will not hurt their children."
- "No, they will not suffer."
- "No, they will never give up."
- "No, sickness will not live in their bodies."
- "No, they will not be financially embarrassed."
- "No, their ministry will not fail."
- "No."
- "No."
- "No."

Jesus' Word carries weight. If He said it, I believe it, and it is coming to pass. You are reading this devotional today because the devil has gotten some NOs concerning your life. God is looking out for you.

#whenJesussaysNo

Day 32
Feeding And Staying

I was feeding my baby girl with some formula one morning, but before I fed her, when she saw the bottle, she motioned towards me, making her hungry sound.

As I sat down, she climbed into my lap, and I placed the bottle in her mouth. She held on to it. When she was full, she took the bottle from her mouth and began to put it in my mouth. I took it from my mouth and gave it back to her. She pushed it away and slid out of my hand, leaving an ounce.

When we were hungry for God, He saw us and sat down to feed us. We grabbed a hold of what He was feeding us. We would not shift a bit; we did not want any to go to waste; neither did we want Him to stop feeding us.

When we thought we had enough, we started pushing things back into God's face. We pushed back His love, His forgiveness, His Word, His blessings, and cleansing, then we slid out of His hands, not realizing that He was not finished feeding us.

Soon, we become weak and hungry again because we did not allow our stomachs to take in the amount prepared for us.

Matthew 5:6
Blessed are those who hunger and thirst for righteousness, for
they will be filled.

Do not get distracted by other things when you are being fed
so that you can be filled to the maximum required capacity; for
there is where your strength lies.

#staying #feeding

Day 33
Access Granted

What is access? Access is the means or opportunity to approach or enter a place; to obtain or retrieve. Which means we can enter the presence of God and obtain all that He has in store for us. Everything we need is already provided and is waiting for us to receive.

Philippians 4:19
And my God will meet all your needs according to the riches of his glory in Christ Jesus.

Sometimes it may seem hard to process this Scripture when we find ourselves in need. It has happened to me, and even as I write, I am experiencing that same feeling where I am growing weary of repeating that Scripture. But I must rule my thoughts and heart, and I am willing myself to believe that His Word is not just for documentation, but are promises to be fulfilled, because He has proven Himself repeatedly. These promises will only be fulfilled on the basis that I follow Him wholeheartedly.

Sometimes I do not understand His Word and what He is saying to me, but everything I need is in His Word. There is a Scripture to explain the Scripture that I do not understand. Whatever I need is in God, and the Word was in the beginning, and the Word was God (See 1 John 1:1). Whatever we need is in Him: wisdom, knowledge, understanding, healing, breakthroughs, financial blessings, companionship, friendship, fellowship; whatever you need: ACCESS GRANTED.

#accessgranted #activatingmyfaithtoliveHispromisedWord
#heavenandearthshallpassbeforeoneofHisWordpass

Day 34
The Process Of Maturity

The online dictionary defines maturity as having reached the most advanced stage in a process. I am still maturing, like so many of us. In the same way an embryo needs nourishment to grow, the process to maturity requires nourishment. Whatever condition we find ourselves in will reflect our growth. While we may come out just the same, there is a great chance that we will be affected by our surroundings. Hence, our growth spurts.

Maturity involves everything in our experiences; we can either grow from them or die literally, socially, psychologically, and spiritually.

Luke 8:14
The seed that fell among thorns stands for those who hear, but as they go on their way they are choked by life's worries, riches and pleasures, and they do not mature.

I have been among thorns that nearly choke the life out of me, but I started growing and blooming to maturity when I got intoxicated with oxygen.

Have patience with yourself and with others. After all, Jesus is still patient with us, and we are still not fully matured.

#betootherswhatJESUSistous

Day 35
Living By God's Qualification

If I were to tell you everything about me, maybe you would not want to read my devotional or hear anything from me. Thank God He knows everything about me, yet He still permits me to share His holy Word.

Some people are familiar with you and what you have done. Some people are aware of your struggles, so they underestimate the work God is doing through you. Avail yourself for His doing just the same.

God knew you then and still knows you are struggling, but He chose you anyway. He is looking for availability, not perfection.

#livingGodsqualifiedchosenlife

Day 36
Living An Unsecured Life

I went to the kitchen to prepare breakfast one morning and saw a tin of milk on the counter with "mini" ants crawling all over it. I was sure some had fallen into it. The milk was used to make tea the night before, and apparently, my husband forgot to put it back in the refrigerator. Luke 11:24-26 is a Scripture that came to mind after observing the scenario: *"When an impure spirit comes out of a person, it goes through arid places seeking rest and does not find it. Then it says, 'I will return to the house I left.' When it arrives, it finds the house swept clean and put in order. Then it goes and takes seven other spirits more wicked than itself, and they go in and live there. And the final condition of that person is worse than the first."*

There are times we get used by the Lord, but afterward, we forget to secure the contents in the preservation covering of Him who used us. We leave ourselves open for all sorts of things to crawl in, things like pride and self-righteousness. We become proud when we think it is who we are that causes Him to use us, thinking of ourselves more highly than we ought to (See Romans 12:3).

When that happens, we flaunt self-righteous attitudes, giving way to the devil to destroy us.

76

Let us not be wise in our own ways but fear the Lord. Be humble enough to know that God has seen us fit to be used as His vessel to demonstrate His work and convey His Word.

Let us secure our containers with the content inside after we have been used by the Lord.

Day 37
Don't Go Back To The Mess!

My baby girl, Hannah, pooped, and I did not realize until she started fussing. Before that, I took her up to feed her. It was a practice of mine to check her diaper regularly, so when I checked, I realized she had pooped. So, I went to change her. In the process of changing her, she kept putting her hands back in the mess, and I continued to take her hands out. 2 Corinthians 5:17 states that: "*...if anyone is in Christ, the new creation has come: The old has gone, the new is here.*" The mess has passed, and you are being cleaned, so forget the mess.

If this is you, God has seen and heard you fussing. He picks you up to start the cleaning process, but you keep putting yourself back in the mess. He is holding your hands, but you keep pulling it away and grabbing on to the mess. Sit still under the cleansing of the Almighty.

Hebrews 6:4-6 reminds us:
It is impossible for those who have once been enlightened, who have tasted the heavenly gift, who have shared in the Holy Spirit, who have tasted the goodness of the word of God and the powers of the coming age and who have fallen away, to be brought back to repentance. To their loss they are crucifying

the Son of God all over again and subjecting him to public disgrace.

For you to stay clean, you must let go of the mess.

Day 38
Doing The Right Thing

I was hanging out some clothes, but the sun was hot, so I took up more clothes in my hand than usual. I went by the line to pin them, but I had to empty my hands to properly pin each garment on the line. I placed the others on the line, and it fell in the dirt. I did not spin dry, so they were still very wet and took up all the dirt. I had to put them in the tub to re-rinse.

I shook my head and hissed my teeth, but as I did, I heard in my thoughts, "You knew it was going to fall off because it is not the first time you did it. It happened just a short while ago with the first set of clothing, so why are you upset when it is your doing."

Hebrews 10:26-29
If we deliberately keep on sinning after we have received the knowledge of the truth, no sacrifice for sins is left, but only a fearful expectation of judgment and of raging fire that will consume the enemies of God. Anyone who rejected the law of Moses died without mercy on the testimony of two or three witnesses. How much more severely do you think someone deserves to be punished who has trampled the Son of God underfoot, who has treated as an unholy thing the blood of the

covenant that sanctified them, and who has insulted the Spirit of grace?

Sometimes we fall in the dirt because of our own willful doing. We know there is a path in life we should not take, yet we run the risk and presumptuously go ahead. We also know that the path we take will not bear us, and it will flip us over because it is not the first we are doing such. When it does flip us over, and we get messed up, we get angry over it; we act as if it is not our fault, and we do not want to be reprimanded about it. We may even go to the extent of defending and justifying what we did, when all we needed to do was stay humble about the matter, accept that we failed to be more responsible, and move straight to get clean.

Do the right thing! Take the right path. If you get dirty, there is water for the cleansing; do not stay dirty. Brush off and rinse again.

Day 39
Who Or What Are We Producing?

I constantly examine the world I live in, and I realize that the world produces its kind every day. Gaza-side produces Gaza artists and Gaza fans; gully-side produces gully artists and gully fans.

I turn my lens to the body of Christ. Are kingdom bearers producing kingdom bearers or are we just reproducing church members for different denominations or reproducing ourselves for self-elevation?

The Bible says we should go into all the world, preach the gospel, and make disciples.

Matthew 28:19-20
Therefore, go and make disciples of all nations, baptizing them in the name of the Father and of the Son and of the Holy Spirit, and teaching them to obey everything I have commanded you. And surely, I am with you always, to the very end of the age.

Whose disciples? Not ours, but Jesus' disciples. Jesus' absence from the world is now seen in us through our lifestyle and actions. If the kingdom of God is near, it means, therefore, that we as kingdom bearers should be reproducing more kingdom bearers.

Who or what are you reproducing?

Day 40
Jesus, My Oxygen

The song, "You are my oxygen" is powerful. It is a song I love very much. But what is oxygen? Oxygen is a colorless, odorless reactive gas; the chemical element of atomic number eight and the life-supporting component of the air. We will stop breathing and die without oxygen.

A stanza in the song says, "Baby steps and short breaths, anything is progress." You, Jesus, sustain my every moment. True, but there is a flip side to the baby steps. If, after a year, the baby does not seem interested in getting mobile, then he or she must be taken to the general practitioner. The brain needs oxygen to function and send signals to the different parts of our bodies.

Anything that is oxygenated grows. If Jesus is our oxygen, it means we should be growing. A seed that is planted in fertile ground that shows no form of growth has nothing to do with the fertile ground but everything to do with the seed.

John 15:5
I am the vine; you are the branches. If you remain in me and I in you, you will bear much fruit; apart from me you can do nothing.

What type of seed are you? A bad seed? A good seed? If you are planted in oxygen (Jesus), you should be growing and excelling in Him. A good seed springs forth, grows into a tree, and produces good fruit. Being at one stage for too long is a clear indication that you are not being affected by the oxygen.

Day 41
God Will Establish You

I had a different feeling some time ago; things are starting to look up now. Things are not altogether in place, but I trust God and what He said in His Word. His promises are yay and amen.

He is not a man that He should lie; He cannot lie. I believe Him, with all my heart, that my tomorrow will be greater than my today and yesterday. He said it perfectly in Jeremiah 29:11: "For I know the plans I have for you," declares the Lord, "plans to prosper you and not to harm you, plans to give you hope and a future." So, I rest surely in His promise.

His plans concerning you will never change, even if you change. Whatever you did not get, or will not get, is because you walked out of the plan. Whatever He promised you, once you come into alignment with Him, it will be yours. It is there untouched, for He will not give it until you are prepared for it. You shall be established.

God's plans for you are secured, with a bright hope and future.

~ Kefira Reid

Day 42
Battle Strategies

W hat causes us to be defeated in battle?

Whenever the children of Israel were faced with a war, the Lord always gave them instructions prior to being engaged: whether they should go or not go or if they would be defeated. In the book of Judges 2:1-4, we see a perfect example of Israel's disobedience: *"The angel of the Lord went up from Gilgal to Bokim and said, "I brought you up out of Egypt and led you into the land I swore to give to your ancestors. I said, 'I will never break my covenant with you, and you shall not make a covenant with the people of this land, but you shall break down their altars.' Yet you have disobeyed me. Why have you done this? And I have also said, 'I will not drive them out before you; they will become traps for you, and their gods will become snares to you.'" When the angel of the Lord had spoken these things to all the Israelites, the people wept aloud."*

Being defeated is not on God; it was a consequence of their disobedience to God. In all instances, when they were defeated, it was because of their rebellion towards God.

Today we are no different from the children of Israel. We lost some battles because of our disobedience to God also; simple battles that could have easily been won. We murmur, grumble, and complain. At times, we are in a battle with the wrong people, not paying attention to the real enemy.

There were times I found myself questioning every instruction because my finite self could not see beyond what He was telling me to do, and, sometimes, it did not seem scientifically possible; neither did it align with my reasoning capabilities. So, in fear, I disregarded what God said because I was afraid to look foolish. Sometimes I went when He did not say go and stayed when He said go.

Remember, our position is down, and He is up. He sees far beyond what we can see. He knows what battles we should engage in and the ones we should walk away from. Prior to us being engaged in battle, He will give us instructions as to how to go about the battle. When we are obedient to God, we are not fighting for victory but in victory.

We have three powerful weapons (prayer, worship, and the Word), which we sometimes trade for a physical or carnal weapon. If we are defeated in battle, it is not because God wants us to be defeated. He allows it because we disobey Him. If the glory of God has departed from us, then we are already fighting a losing battle.

Day 43
Being Tactical

One Saturday, I packed the baby's bag, put it in arms reach so as not to forget it when we were heading out, and a few hours later, we were on our way to a function.

We hit the highway, took the payment card for the toll road, and something hit me; I asked if the bag was taken up. "No," was the reply. Oh, the rage I felt on the inside. We could not turn back as there was no way to turn back on that road. We had to continue driving until we reached a turn off, then go back through a toll to retrieve the bag.

We had to go back. Why?

1. Everything for the baby was in the bag: formula, diapers, change of clothing, bottles, wipes, you name it, all was in the bag.

2. The baby needed changing.

3. We did not take extra money to buy all the missing stuff in the bag, which would have been too much on our pockets anyway.

Before you go about your daily lives, ensure you pack everything you need to sustain you for the journey. Ensure that you are stocked up on prayer and the fruit of the Spirit (love, joy, peace, forbearance, kindness, goodness, faithfulness, gentleness, and self-control). Luke 21:36 tells us that we should always be alert. Pray so you have the power to escape everything that is about to happen and to stand in front of the Son of Man. It is not someone else's responsibility. Do not wait until you get halfway through your journey before you realize that all I mentioned above is needed. Turning back will delay how far you could have been.

When you meet upon the works of the flesh, you should already be prepared. Do not just prepare these attributes, bring them along with you wherever you go, so they can be easily activated when the need arises.

Day 44
Blocked Up

WhWhat are you blocked up with?

Romans 12:2
Do not conform to the pattern of this world but be transformed
by the renewing of your mind. Then you will be able to test and
approve what God's will is—his good, pleasing, and perfect
will.

I remember two consecutive nights, my baby girl had difficulty
sleeping because her nostrils were blocked due to having a
cold. I gave her nasal spray and DPH. It helped for a while, but
then it got blocked again. In the mornings, I noticed that the
mucus ran out. My next option was to use the nasal pump to
pull out the mucus, but I could not find it. I decided to let it run
out naturally.

What is causing you sleepless nights? What has blocked your
thoughts and inner peace?

Maybe the temporary reliefs you are applying are not working.
Whatever you need to do to keep healthy, do it. If it means
getting rid of old habits, do it; dropping some friends, do it.
Maybe it is what you read, watch, or engage in. The Word of

God applied will allow what is blocking to run out until you are able to breathe freely again.

A blocked mind contributes to sleepless nights. A healthy mind contributes to a healthy heart, which connects with a healthy spirit.

~ *Kefira Reid*

Day 45
Squeezed

I was doing laundry one day, and I looked at the washer. It was looking good on the outside; the water was filling up to its selected point, and it was about to rinse. The problem was, at the end of the rinse, I had to squeeze the water from the clothes before hanging them on the line because a part of the inside of the tub was broken. Maybe I overloaded it or underloaded, if that is a word, but the rinse and spin cycle was not working.

Isaiah 41:10
So do not fear, for I am with you; do not be dismayed, for I am your God. I will strengthen you and help you; I will uphold you with my righteous right hand.

Many Christians go to church, read their Bibles, and get filled up with the Word, but are unable to let it out to affect people's lives because we are broken. We are overloaded with the cares of the world, or the pride of life and actions bury the substance we have. If and when we do let out, it is not enough to bring about a difference, so sometimes God has to keep us at a place where He can squeeze out the potential, squeeze out the gift, squeeze out the abilities so we can be effective.

When we are being squeezed in our brokenness, all the unpleasantness will come out, but when we surrender to God and are being squeezed, others will experience His goodness.

Colossians 3:12-14
Therefore, as God's chosen people, holy and dearly loved, clothe yourselves with compassion, kindness, humility, gentleness, and patience. Bear with each other and forgive one another if any of you has a grievance against someone. Forgive as the Lord forgave you. And over all these virtues put on love, which binds them all together in perfect unity.

The squeeze is not to hurt you; it is to bring out the best in you. Do not just get filled up; squeeze out and change the world.

Day 46
Staying The Course

While heading home one evening, halfway in the journey, we got caught in a long line of traffic. When I checked the time, it was 7:05 PM. We finally got home at 10 PM. What caught my attention was the behaviors of the different commuters on the road.

There was a lane for going and one for coming, but then I realized that persons were being impatient and destructive; they undertook, overtook, and even interjected the other vehicles. In a short space of time, we had to be swerving to not get hit or hit anyone, pulling sudden brakes and all. Those who were in the wrong shouted, "Come out the way," while forcefully squeezing in front of us and other vehicles. At one point, we had to allow another vehicle to proceed ahead of us as he was completely in the road, obstructing the oncoming traffic.

In all this chaotic situation, my husband kept his composure. He stayed in his lane and stayed on course. I had a little road rage because I wanted to get out of the traffic, and to see other impatient, unruly people cheat their way ahead made me a little flustered.

Isaiah 26:3
You will keep in perfect peace those whose minds are steadfast, because they trust in you.

On this journey to get home to glory, we will be faced with many challenges and obstacles. You will find others undertaking and overtaking you. At some point, it will seem as if they are obstructing you and even criticize you for being on the right track.

There will be days when you must stop and put others in front of you in order for them not to cause any collision and hurt their own selves. The temptation may arise to give over to rage. In all that is happening, stay your course.

Proverbs 4:25
Let your eyes look straight ahead; fix your gaze directly before you.

Keep your eyes on the journey. It may seem long, but in a matter of time, you will reach your destination.

With every distraction, stay your course.
~ Kefira Reid

Day 47
Be Prepared! Stay Ready!

One morning, the security called to inform me that there was someone at the gate. After I hung up, I looked around to see if my living room was in order. I woke up fifteen minutes prior because all my kids were up, even the baby (as if she were going to school).

I closed the door to the boy's room because I thought what was going to be done would have been in the living area, only to find out that the work would be done throughout the entire house. I was frightened because it was early, and one of the boys was yet to be looked after to go out, and nothing was done in the house. I started moving about, moving bits and pieces out of the way; kid's stuff, sweeping away visible dirt so it could look presentable. The bottom line, my house was unprepared for a guest. He waited while I hurriedly move about.

My thoughts flashed back to the story told of the ten virgins. Five were wise, and five were foolish; the wise virgins were ready and prepared, while the foolish virgins were unprepared and not ready (See Matthew 25:1-13). God is not going to wait on us until we clean up. He has been giving us time. He did warn us that He is coming back again. He did not say when, but we must be prepared. Stay prepared! We cannot afford to forget His Word and promise to return for a people who have their minds set on Him. We cannot afford to only have one part of our lives in order while the other part has a closed-door because there is a mess and unkempt situations. Fixing up the outer part so people can see how well put together we are is not going to cut it.

When Jesus makes His unannounced return, it is for immediate effect. He is not going to call and tell us He is on His way. He is not going through security; He is the Security. As a Security, He has the power to let through anyone He sees fit to enter through the gate.

If you are not prepared, now is the time to get ready. We should have already been swept clean and waiting. If you are prepared, then stay prepared because Scripture says in Habakkuk 2:3: *"For the revelation awaits an appointed time; it speaks of the end and will not prove false. Though it linger, wait for it; it will certainly come and will not delay."*

Day 48
Trust God With Everything

A conversation under a mango tree in the cool evening can spark quite an interesting eye-opener. So, hubby and I were talking on the matter of Christians trusting God. We said a lot, but I will share one thing that was the highlight of our talk. When we are faced with circumstances, and we hear God telling us to trust Him, we gladly say yes, we will trust Him. God is infinite, and He sees our whole life ahead of us. While He is telling us to trust Him, He is not saying to trust Him only for this leg of the struggle, but for the ones that are coming that are much bigger than what we see.

Very often, after the small problem is over, we never anticipate the others that are coming. So, trust goes through the window because we were only focusing on the now. We need to know that when God says to trust Him, He is talking for a lifetime: little, medium, or big circumstances. He is not just asking us to trust Him when we think a situation is manageable, but even when it is beyond human capacity.

Psalm 37:4-6
Take delight in the Lord, and he will give you the desires of your heart. Commit your way to the Lord; trust in him and he

*will do this: He will make your righteous reward shine like the
dawn, your vindication like the noonday sun.*

*Do not trust God with things we think are manageable; trust
Him with all things. He is in charge of our future.*
~ Kefira Reid

Day 49
Activate Your Connection

There were some lights switched on in the house, so I turned them off. I thought of something, so in my mind, I switched them on again. For the lights to come on, there must be a connection. Turning off the lights did not erase the connection; what it simply needs is a touch or click.

I reflected on my day in church the day before and the number of issues leading up to the point of me being at church. At one point, I decided in my mind that I would just not show up. But I could not be bothered with people texting and calling my phone, asking if I was okay or why I did not come to church. Then again, I was the choir director. They could sing without a choir director, but I had a part to play in that song. I had already made a promise to God that irrespective of my feelings, I would always honor Him to the best of my ability, so I did.

The moment I arrived at church and knelt at the altar, my switch got clicked. All the feelings I had disappeared the moment I entered His presence. His presence filled my soul, and the burdens were lifted. It is true: things change when your relationship with Jesus is not just a mere contact; thoughts and action get shifted, plans rearranged, and feelings subjected to the authority of Christ.

John 15:4
Remain in me, as I also remain in you. No branch can bear fruit by itself; it must remain in the vine. Neither can you bear fruit unless you remain in me.

Your light may have been switched off for various reasons, but if you have a relationship with Jesus, your connection is still there. Coming in contact is not the same as having a connection. You can lose contact, but a connection is always linked between the port, connector (Jesus), and the plug (us). Activate your connection.

It is not just to connect to Jesus but staying in connection with Him changes everything.

~ Kefira Reid

Day 50
Your Transaction Is Being Processed!

I went to the ATM to get some cash because I really needed the money. As I started the transaction, it showed me an inscription that said: "Please insert your card." I did as it asked, then another message came: "Please enter your pin code." I did. Another message came: "Select the amount." I did that too. After I had done all of that, the ATM showed me a message in bold letters: "YOUR TRANSACTION IS BEING PROCESSED. PLEASE WAIT!"

Likewise, you have followed all these instructions, entering your access code by prayer, entered your pin with fasting, yet it seems nothing is coming out. Wait patiently! Do not give up. Do not move because your request is being processed. Wait! Let me tell you what made me wait: my card was already in the ATM. I had already entered my pin code. If I gave up and walked away, the next person would have gotten all that I had requested.

Do not think you are punching in your request, and it is not being attended to. Do not think your prayer requests are irrelevant. Do not think your fasting is meaningless. They are not! Your transaction is being processed.

Psalm 27:14
Wait for the Lord; be strong and take heart and wait for the Lord.

Romans 8:25
But if we hope for what we do not yet have, we wait for it patiently.

The wait may seem long, but it is coming; you will get your receipt one day.

Your processing may be long, but you are just about finished. Wait a little more.

~ Kefira Reid

Day 51
Be Still

Have you ever found yourself in situations that you really want to address, but every time you attempt to address it, you become speechless? For a period, I found myself wanting to react to situations but found that I could not. Every attempt I made was shot down, not by me, but by the Holy Spirit. The Spirit rebukes, exhorts, and edifies. I was being rebuked. I tried to do it in many forms, but they were not forthcoming.

Being still means to listen; be calm, and do not make a sound. If we are being still, we should not be paying attention to what is happening in and around us but have our eyes fixed on Him.

Psalm 46:10
He says, "Be still, and know that I am God; I will be exalted among the nations, I will be exalted in the earth."

"Be still" is an instruction we often refuse to follow because we want to take things into our own hands. When we are still, we will discover the goodness and greatness of the Lord.

1 Samuel 12:16
Now then, stand still and see this great thing the Lord is about to do before your eyes!

I was sitting alone outside my church one Sunday, having a conversation with the Lord. I heard Him clearly say: "Be still and see." I am not sure what I was looking for, but I took that as an assurance. When I got home, and the feelings began to rise again, I started talking to God again, pacing back and forth and doing things to get my mind off everything. I could not help but shed some tears to release some of the tension that was building up.

Another morning, I rose with the same prayer and the same feeling of wanting my prayers answered. Still pacing back and forth in the room, I began to speak to my Father. He spoke again: "Didn't I tell you to be still? Do you remember how stubborn Pharaoh was? Wasn't it so that I could do a marvelous thing in the eyes of all Israel? Be still in your intensity for I, the Lord, will work a work that every man will see that I am He who has acted."

It has proven fruitful for me when I obey God's instructions. He has never instructed me on a matter and left me hanging, and even though it may not be how I wanted it to be handled with my bias and selfish self, His handling it is always better. If He is telling you to be still, obey. You will not always follow with the storyline, but in this movie, the star has never, will never, and can never die.

Be still!

Day 52
The Lord's Covering Beautifies

I was walking by my bathroom door one morning, and as I glanced inside, I could not help but see the nakedness of the floor, so bland and lacking in beauty because I had taken out the mats that so colorfully decorated that area. I had not placed a mat in there since my son messed around with the pipe, which got fixed the day prior, so I was excited to play house again. Looking in, I said, "Wow, this is how we are without the covering of God: bland, naked, and unattractive."

A covering is a thing used to protect, decorate, or conceal something else.

Psalm 5:11
But let all who take refuge in you be glad; let them ever sing for joy. Spread your protection over them, that those who love your name may rejoice in you.

God is not a thing; He is our covering.

Psalm 46:1
God is our refuge and strength, an ever-present help in trouble.

God is our refuge and strength in times of trouble, and He is our covering. He covers our nakedness, shame, and reproach. He beautifies us with His salvation and calls us blessed.

Ezekiel 16:8
Later I passed by, and when I looked at you and saw that you were old enough for love, I spread the corner of my garment over you and covered your naked body. I gave you my solemn oath and entered into a covenant with you, declares the Sovereign Lord, and you became mine.

What happened that caused us to take off the covering of God from over us is not important. What matters is that we recognize how exposed and risky it is to be living without His covering and draw it back on us. His love covering us is like no other, no husband, wife, children, or parents. His covering of forgiveness is comparable to none; He remembers our errors no more. His covering of protection is like no other; He is great and mighty and mighty in battle.

Psalm 32:1-2
Blessed is the one whose transgressions are forgiven; whose sins are covered. Blessed is the one whose sin the Lord does not count against them and in whose spirit is no deceit.

Stay under His covering where character, beauty, love, and protection can be seen by those who see you.

God's covering does not come with mishaps; His work is always completed and well done.

~ Kefira Reid

Day 53
A Renewed Mind

The mind is not to be confused with the brain; it is a set of cognitive faculties, including consciousness, imagination, perception, thinking, judgment, language, and memory. It is usually defined as the faculty of an entity's thoughts and consciousness.

The mind is an immensely powerful tool. We must be careful what we let into it. I can tell you from experience that what you feed the mind will eventually play out. If you go about speculating about people and things, you will eventually see them in the light of your mind because they are stored in the subconscious of your mind. Good, bad, or ugly, if we have not dealt with the issues that plagued us, they become dreams, which will seem like a confirmation of a truth we think we know.

Dr. Caroline Leaf says this in her book, *Switch On Your Brain:* "As we think, we change the physical nature of our brain. As we consciously direct our thinking, we can wire out toxic patterns of thinking and replace them with healthy thoughts."

If there is ill-feeling against someone, chances are our thoughts are not going to be pure. I have often said we become what we practice. Our thoughts are going to generate actions.

110

I remember standing at one of my food places waiting on the food when a forty-leg (worm) ran on my foot. I was so frightened that I ran out in the road without even looking. After I got the food, I went to choir rehearsal and sat down at the bandstand when I felt something burning on my knee. I rubbed it but realized it was still burning so I looked down and there it was: a forty-leg, only this time it bit me. From that day, whenever I feel crawling on me, I think it is a forty-leg, and my reaction is still the same: I stamp and run. Sometimes it is just a grass straw brushing on my leg.

Romans 12:2
Do not conform to the pattern of this world but be transformed by the renewing of your mind. Then you will be able to test and approve what God's will is—his good, pleasing, and perfect will.

2 Corinthians 5:10
For we must all appear before the judgment seat of Christ, so that each of us may receive what is due us for the things done while in the body, whether good or bad.

Watch your thoughts, watch your thoughts, what they think; watch your thoughts, watch your thoughts, or you will sink. For if we dwell on what is bad, they will, in turn, make us sad, watch your thoughts, watch your thoughts, what they think. (KTR).

Philippians 4:8
Finally, brothers and sisters, whatever is true, whatever is noble, whatever is right, whatever is pure, whatever is lovely, whatever is admirable—if anything is excellent or praiseworthy—think about such things.

Day 54
Know Who And Whose You Are

I have been among people who allowed me to feel less than who I am. A feeling of inferiority would sweep over me, and I lose confidence. When these things happen, I become dumbstruck and timid. But when the Holy Spirit gets ahold of me and starts to build His confidence in me, I denounce fear knowing who I belong to and who I am.

Do not feel bad when people put you down, block you, unfriend you, or talk whack about you; they may even go as far as recruiting others in disliking you, wanting them to avoid you. Sometimes what God is doing in your life is making them mad. They will not be able to look at you without a feeling of envy, but you must know whose you are, who you are, where you are going, and what you were sent for. One thing I can encourage you to do, from experience, is pray always for them, asking God to release peace in their hearts; pray for their success and coverage, and all things good.

Do not try to find out answers to a maze of uncertain behaviors. It will only bring you around in a circle, making you confused and all. Let God handle it. We mess things up when we proceed to handle things ourselves. Even in the very mess we find ourselves; look again, something beautiful is growing out of it.

Believe God's declaration over your life and walk in it.
~ Kefira Reid

Day 55
God's Returns Are Greater Than What You Lost

Billy Graham said, "God never takes away something from you without replacing it with something better." I strongly believe that if I am going to reach others effectively, then what I say must not just be word of mouth, but what I have experienced. Theory alone will not give you understanding unless the practicality of the same is exercised.

There are countless stories I can relate that is not just what people say but what I have experienced for myself. I will share a few with you, so you know that God's Word is yes and amen. He did not only replace materially but holistically too. I will try to see how I can consolidate the long post, but just to warn you, we can never be done when talking about God's goodness and blessings. The songwriter rightly pens it, "To write the love of God above would drain the ocean dry."

I will start with the emotional and spiritual aspects. While growing up, I was very unstable: emotionally, physically, and spiritually. I was labeled most likely to fail. I did encounter some failures, but God remained faithful and true to His Word, so His promises took root in my life and brought me out. I was physically unstable as I moved around a lot, seeking refuge at the most suitable place at the time. There were times when I stayed at my pastor's house, and there were times I would stay with friends. Sometimes I would be at my mother's house until I took permanent residence with my sister, whom I love dearly. Emotionally, I was a mess. Circumstances surrounding my emotional mess steered me in the path where psychological help was sought for me because of my state. I only did two sessions. The doctor was not getting anywhere with me, so she called it quits. Spiritually, I was fluctuating as the pressures of life weighed me down. I struggled to find my place in God, struggled with the uncertainty of God's love for and towards me. I shunned God's love for me and restrained myself from experiencing any goodness and favour extended to me. I would shun prayer because I thought myself less than I ought to, comparing myself to others and how they were Godly, and thinking I was not a part of the chosen.

Thanks be to God, He brought me out. The midnight came to an end when He reached into the miry clay, took me, all broken and bruised, placed me on His turning wheel, and made me over. Hallelujah! God replaced my emotional, spiritual, and physical instability with His renewed Spirit, gave me a family, and a renewed mind where I could groom healthy emotions.

To start listing the material blessings will take a while. I will share two examples of how God replaced better for what was taken away. Between my husband and I, we have had four phones taken from us. How they were taken is a whole other story! The first was a Huawei; we both had the same phones, those were taken. They got replaced with Samsung galaxies.

They were taken and got replaced with iPhones. Are you telling me that God does not stay true to His Word?

For years we did ministry without having any transportation. We would sit for hours waiting on taxis to take us to and from church and go about our daily lives. Sometimes we would walk long miles to and from church; the heels from my shoes would eat away. My shoe closet is another story. My sister-in-law, who is my husband's sister, had a little car we called "Betsy." She gave it to us to help with our mobilization, but Betsy started acting up; breaking down with us on the road, even at gas stations. I remember once we went to a convention in Old Harbour, and it broke down at the traffic stop. I wanted to melt. We encountered many embarrassing moments, but we stayed faithful to God.

After two years, God replaced Betsy with a brand-new Toyota Rav 4. Are you still trying to convince me He does not do what He said He would do? I could go on and on.

God's Word in Philippians 4:19 says: *"And my God will meet all your needs according to the riches of his glory in Christ Jesus."*

In Matthew 6:30, Jesus said, *"If that is how God clothes the grass of the field, which is here today and tomorrow is thrown into the fire, will he not much more clothe you—you of little faith?"*

Our duty is not to worry about where, how, who, when or what He is going to use to bless us; all we need to do is to be faithful to Him, and He will reward us for our faithfulness.

If you are experiencing midnight, your morning is coming; if it is rain, your sunshine is coming; if it is dark clouds, your clear sky is coming. Do not have a fit over what you have lost because His returns are far greater.

Day 56
Fixing The Leakage In Our Lives

I can never love God enough. I really appreciate the way He has timely formed everyone and placed within them unique abilities to get His work done. Everybody is useful to the kingdom. God deliberately creates scenarios for me to learn His ways and apply His Word.

One Thursday, at the break of dawn, I had a vision: I was in the bathroom, and I had one of Elj's shirts in my hand, but somehow it fell in the toilet as it was being flushed. It blocked the passage, causing it to overflow. There was a man there who had to pull the bowl out to get the shirt. While he did, it created a mess. I then woke up.

My husband took my younger son from school early that day to run some errands. He came home, did what he had to do, and went outside to play. I saw him enter the bathroom but did not see when he got out. About an hour or so after, he went into the bathroom again, this time he came out saying, "Mommy, the bathroom is flooded."

"What," I said. I got up to look. I checked to see if he had tampered with the bowl, but it was good. I checked to see if he turned on the bath pipe and left it on, but that was not it. I stooped down and saw that the water was dripping from the

119

toilet lock off. He was playing with it so much that it got spoilt, and I had to tighten it. Despite that, it was still dripping. I had to place a container underneath to catch the drippings whenever I turn it on for the tank to be filled.

I laughed; really, I did. At that moment I was wondering what God was coming with this time. Was He telling me that I needed a new house, a change of fixtures, or was He telling me what a leakage in our lives could result in? Let us look at some definitions of a leak.

As a verb, a leak means to accidentally lose or admit contents, especially liquid or gas, through a hole or crack or secret information made known.

As a noun, a leak means a hole in a container or covering through which contents may accidentally pass or an intentional disclosure of secret information.

The possible reasons for a leak vary, such as foundational shifts. Small shifts in our homes can create big adjustments in our water lines, causing them to disconnect or rupture. Corrosion is damage caused to materials that are usually of an older version. Then there is the temperature changes. An extreme change in temperature can cause pipes to crack and leak. It is also important to note that leakages that are not controlled or fixed result in rusts overtime. For us to prevent leakage, control of these factors is a must.

Let me also establish in this context that this leakage I am referring to is a waste. Now that we have discovered what a leak is, and the possible reasons for a leak, and have established that it can be accidental or intentional, let us now make the application to our lives.

Let us look at Jeremiah 2:13: "My people have committed two sins: they have forsaken me, the spring of living water, and have dug their own cisterns, broken cisterns that cannot hold water."

The children of Israel had the full resources of God, the living water, but turned to other gods that could not fill their longing because those gods were broken, empty, and unable to provide for their spiritual needs or provide for them holistically. When I turn away from the foundation of my faith, Jesus, it means I am now connecting with some other source, which will corrode the channel through which I get living, clean and sustainable water. When this corrosion happens, I will experience leakage; leakage will have me being rusty. Now the works of the flesh which are these: adultery, fornication, uncleanness, lasciviousness, idolatry, witchcraft, hatred, variance, emulations, wrath, strife, seditions, heresies, envying, murders, drunkenness, reveling and such like. (Galatians 5:19-21). These will end up damaging my entire being.

Remember, the Bible tells us that our body is the temple of God (1 Corinthians 6:19-20); therefore, an intentional or accidental leak will destroy the very house that the Lord wants to reside in. A damaged house will end up costing a fortune to fix but thank God it costs us nothing, but it did cost the original owner of the house everything: His life for mine. Accidental or intentional leakage lowers the value of a product; we do not want to lower the value on Jesus Christ in us; neither do we want it to cost us dearly in the long run.

Many times, along our Christian journey, the leakages are unintentional, but the damage caused is great. Serious health and hazardous situations are also the result of this unattended leakage. Sometimes we are the ones who did the damage but fail to correct it. Whether we are preoccupied with other things or the leakage is pointed out to us by someone else, let us fix our leaking pipes. Let us put up our sign: "Caution! Wet floor ahead" to prevent any accidents. Let us get to fixing. If the hose needs changing, do accordingly. Whatever it is, fix the leak.

Day 57
Rebrand! Remodel! Refocus!

Romans 8:6
The mind governed by the flesh is death, but the mind governed by the Spirit is life and peace.

1 Timothy 4:16
Watch your life and doctrine closely. Persevere in them, because if you do, you will save both yourself and your hearers.

One night I woke up to go to the bathroom, stood at the door, and I heard God speak. It was so clear. I went and asked my husband for the meaning. The prefix "re" simply means "again."

Rebrand: change the corporate image of a company or organization.

Remodel: shape a figure or object again or differently.

Refocus: adjust the focus of a lens or one's eyes.

Whatever God speaks, even one word, transcends beyond my limited understandings and will cause me to learn and grow from it for years.

1 Peter 5:10
And the God of all grace, who called you to his eternal glory in Christ, after you have suffered a little while, will himself restore you and make you strong, firm and steadfast.

Drawing attention to my present state, I see where God is pointing me to this rebranding, remodeling, and refocusing as it relates to my faith, marriage, children, and the issue of kingdom advancement.

The fact that He says "re" is an indication that it was there before but had stopped or detoured from the original masterpiece. It is a wake-up call to open our eyes to see where we have drifted and to find our place in Him; to conduct ourselves in such a way that will draw attention to God's kingdom and not to ourselves and help prepare the bride of Christ.

Our daily social living must reflect that of Christ and should never be lived by our own standards, belief or structure; be it in marriage, growing our children or living among people.

Colossians 3:10
And have put on the new self, which is being renewed in knowledge in the image of its Creator.

It is a time of introspection, evaluation, and application. Start the process.

Day 58
Getting Rid Of The Garbage

I was sitting in my living room one day during playtime with Hannah. I was focused on what she was watching and joined her. I had my back door open, like always, so fresh air could filter in. I got up to get her some juice, and I saw a cat running from my kitchen. I went after it, and it dashed out.

When I came back to the kitchen, I realized that it bit the bag that had the garbage, and some of the disposables fell to the floor, causing an ant raid. I took down the bag, tied it up, and properly disposed of it in the garbage disposal provided for the collectors to pick up.

Mark 7:20-23
He went on: "What comes out of a person is what defiles them. For it is from within, out of a person's heart, that evil thoughts come—sexual immorality, theft, murder, adultery, greed, malice, deceit, lewdness, envy, slander, arrogance and folly. All these evils come from inside and defile a person."

In our Christian journey, there is a need to leave the doors to our hearts and minds open for the Holy Spirit to breathe freshness into it. If we do not dispose of the garbage inside daily, then it is going to attract the predators (the devil), who is going to bite at it, and scatter it all over where other people will gather to discover our dirt and stench, dragging it all over the place to create a bigger mess. When we leave our door open, we must ensure we watch, so the enemy cannot come in and find stuff to scatter and accuse us. Scripture says it this way: "…be transformed by the renewing of your mind… ." (Romans 12:2).

Day 59
God Will Disrupt Anything That Takes His Attention!

Isaiah 51:4
Listen to me, my people; hear me, my nation: instruction will go out from me; my justice will become a light to the nations.

My daughter sat on my lap as I shared what I was eating with her. She was watching her favorite programs on the screen. I realized that each time the food was out of her mouth, she would turn and hold on to me. When I was not attending to her, she would push the phone out my hand, and if I try taking it up again, she would repeat the same with mumblings. I thought, "Wow, this is exactly what God has been showing me."

We are earthly beings, and we have things that occupy our time, such as work, relationships, children, business, or whatever it is. Yet, at times, God will push some of these things out of our hands so He can get our attention. We were created for His pleasure, and when He sees that we are falling short, He must disrupt our lives to get us back on track.

Pay attention! He keeps pushing things out of place for us to recognize that our priorities and focus are detracted. When our focus is on Him, everything else will fall into place.

Day 60
Don't Hide It, Tell It

My eldest son went to close the back door some minutes after 6 PM one evening. During the days, a piece of granite countertop is used to keep the door from closing. At 8:07 PM, I went outside to fetch something and stepped in a puddle of water. I looked in astonishment as I wondered where this pool of water could be coming from. I heard the sound of a mighty rushing river. I looked to the side of the washtub but still could not see where the water was coming from until I looked to my right, and there it was: a water fountain gushing out from the hot water pipe. I did not draw any conclusions about what had happened or what could possibly be the reason for that water outburst. I turned to go back inside, wondering if it was the water pressure.

I asked my son, "What happened?" He said he was going to tell me, but he was afraid. Eventually, he did. I was so mad, I scolded him, not because he threw the granite on the pipe, which he said was an accident, but because instead of letting me know so I could turn the main off and not have water wasting away and flooding the yard, he locked the door knowing what he did, and left the water running for over two hours. I was anticipating a huge water bill.

Another thing that hit me was the fact that he said he was afraid to tell me. I always said I wanted my kids to tell me everything, even when it was bad, but I discovered that the relationship had not yet grown to that point, so he was afraid to tell me. That is something I must work on.

Then it hit me again: so it is with us. Whenever we fall into wrongdoing, instead of going to God so He can rectify the problem, we hide it from Him, not knowing that He knows and He sees. When we refuse to confess to Him, the sin goes up His nostrils, and He is going to call us out on it. It does not matter if it was an accidental occurrence; what He wants from us is honesty and transparency in our daily walk with Him. This is called relationship.

Romans 1:18
The wrath of God is being revealed from heaven against all the godlessness and wickedness of people, who suppress the truth by their wickedness.

Hiding our mistakes from God will only enhance the punishment we were to receive in the beginning. Being the loving God that He is, He does not always punish us as our sins deserve (See Psalm 103:10), but because we proceed to cover up, even when we know we are to confess, we end up getting the full punishment and more.

An accidental occurrence is not an indication to hide from God. He knows all things; He knows we are prone to mistakes and failures; He knows how frail we are, but He requires that we be blameless by not hiding from Him, which we cannot do. He wants us to have a relationship with Him where we can be free to say when we have messed up.

Proverbs 28:13
Whoever conceals their sins does not prosper, but the one who confesses and renounces them finds mercy.

God is not like us. He has a listening ear, a responsive heart, loving attributes, and a forgiving arm that restores us to righteousness. Do not hide it; tell it.

A healthy relationship includes honesty and openness.
~ Kefira Reid

Day 61
You Will Survive The Valley

A valley is a long depression or ditch in the earth's surface. It usually lies between the ranges of hills or mountains. Most valleys are formed by rivers that erode or wear down soil and rocks. This process takes thousands or millions of years. There is a song which says, *"When I'm low in Spirit I cry Lord lift me up. I want to go higher with thee. But the Lord knows I can't live on a mountain. So He picked out a valley for me. It's dark as a dungeon, and the sun seldom shines, and I question, Lord, why must this be? But He tells me, there's strength in my sorrow, and there's victory in trials for me."*

I have been singing this song for years; riding on the music and singing with eyes closed. One morning the song really reached into my innermost being. I have encountered lows in my spirit before, been in dungeons, and had lonely pathways, but as I sat down with tears streaming down my face that day, the song came to me, and instead of singing it, I spoke the words and listened as I spoke the words.

God will disrupt the things that take away His attention. I realize that God has disrupted some things in my life, and they have plunged me into the valley. There were days I was on the mountain, but I was getting too comfortable, so He allowed

131

things to happen that brought me to the valley. In the valley, I have no choice but to call on His name and seek His face. I have no choice but to focus my attention on Him and Him only.

In those valley moments, it is very dark and filled with dry bones. At that moment, I have no hope for the best because of the intensity of the test. In those moments, I do not want to be asked if these dry bones can live; all I want is to get on the mountain.

In my hopelessness, darkness, and dysfunctional state, He is letting me know that He will restore my soul.

Psalm 62:8
Trust in him at all times, you people; pour out your hearts to him, for God is our refuge.

My salvation and honor depend on God. He is my mighty Rock, my Refuge. As He begins to restore my soul, a scab is forming. If you have ever done biology, you know the scab's job is to protect the cut by keeping germs and other stuff out and giving the skin cells underneath a chance to heal. White blood cells also get rid of any dead blood and skin cells that may still be hanging around the cut.

I am not completely healed yet. This time it is not a white blood cell that is getting rid of any of the dead blood or skin; it is the crimson red blood of the crucified Savior. He is making a transfusion in my body, and soon I will be oxygenated and ready to live again.

Your valley may be filled with dry bones, dark clouds, drought, famine, in whichever area of your life, but know that restoration is coming. Do not worry about the scab; it may look ugly, but it is necessary. Do not worry about the transfusion process; you will experience symptoms from the procedure but know that you have been given a second chance at life. Valley experiences are rough and tough, but you will survive because He has built us to survive. You will be restored!

Even in our valley, we can bloom because Jesus is the river that runs through; He will water our roots.

~ Kefira Reid

Day 62
Sometimes Our Struggles Repeat Itself

Quitting is a word I have used so often; it has become cliché. In every level of my life, I have thought about quitting: my job, family, marriage, church, and sometimes faith. In those lonely dark moments, I do not have clarity of thought, so my thoughts reflect my actions.

In my earlier years of ministry, I never really knew what I was to do as I never really took the time to avail myself in any capacity to see my capabilities. I knew I could sing and considered singing as my area of gifting. I was wrong. Singing is not a gift; it is more of a learned skill or a natural talent. So, I would sing here and there but still had not found out which area of ministry the Lord would have me function in.

Fast forward into the now, and I am discovering where He wants me to serve. I am now functioning in three capacities: Worship Leader/Coordinator, Choir Director, and Women's Ministries President, the last one was not my choice, but God be praised anyhow. Every now and again, I hurt, I bleed, and I heal, and the same repeats itself. In each given case, when I am healing, I find that the ugly things are seen on top. It is like getting a bottle that is filled with dirt and pouring water into it; the dirt surfaces. What is coming out is all the dirt, but cleaning is taking place. So, when Jesus is pouring His Word into me, I am getting cleaned, and all the undesirables and ugly matter are coming out, and that is what is seen, but healing is taking place.

I quit the Women's Ministry a million times; the choir another million, not to mention worship because when all the undesirables are coming out, I am at a place where I think I am not worthy of leading. In those times, I just drag myself to church, unmotivated, even after preparation for the task. But because I have been given an office to function in, I must fill my obligations to the given office.

When I am at my lowest, God gets the best out of me. In those lows, when I am not operating off my own strength and capabilities, that is when God gets selfless worship, and that is when He gets the glory out of me. He is in control of me in my quitting state; my reins are let loose, and He is having His way with me as He leads me into the different aspects of the given task.

The temptation to quit is enticing as we seem to gather all the reasons to justify quitting. They may even sound and look justifiable, but it is better to struggle in whatever capacity God has placed you until you master the art of working under strenuous circumstances. He will enable us to do whatever He has called us to do, and He has already made provisions to get them done. It may be the easiest thing to do, but do not quit.

Day 63
Learn The Boundaries And Close The Door

On many occasions, I have swept my living room with the doors opened at the back and front. 99.99% of the time, I know that the wind is going to blow it back. When that happens, I get so worked up and mad about it, sometimes asking God if He did not see me sweeping and why He waited till I was sweeping to blow the wind. What I should have done was close the door, sweep the dirt into the scoop or to the door where it could easily go outside.

God created His world, and He has put everything in place to accommodate and sustain us. He set the time frame and boundaries for creation, so instead of having a fit over what we cannot change, our only option is to adjust ourselves to the foundation of the things He created and work with their functions.

I am familiar with how people function: how they think, how they behave, and what their responses will be in a given scenario, but I still go ahead and push an engagement in an unfiltered conversation, which results in it blowing up in my face. At that point, I get worked up about wanting a different outcome when it was my responsibility to make the necessary preparations before engaging in any form of confrontation. I often know the boundaries to which I am allowed to go but still try to go beyond it.

It is not our place to change anything in or about anyone. God created people, and all the changes they will ever need to make are solely dependent on them and their choices. When God created us, He gave us the ability to make wise decisions. Let us not leave our doors open when we know the wind is always blowing. Recognize the direction the wind is coming from and know when to close a door; a door to an unpleasant argument; a door to a situation that produces no fruit and ugly outcomes. You know the function of the wind, so close the door.

Day 64
Jesus The Absolute Truth
(Cone Of Truth)

I took a nap with my daughter a little after 2 PM one day. It seemed I was dreaming when I heard "Cone of truth." I immediately got up. I began turning over those words in my head repeatedly, even thinking about ice-cream.

Then I decided to look up "cone." It was then that my head got so excited with information that I started using my word pad just to remember some of the things I was getting. A cone is a three-dimensional geometric shape that tapers smoothly from a flat base to a point called the apex or vertex. An apex is the highest part of something forming a point, which is the same definition for a vertex.

Jesus said, "I am the way, the truth, and the life" (See John 14:6). The "cone of truth" is three-dimensional or what we call the Trinity: Father, Son, and Holy Spirit. How does this apply to us now? I was hearing that God is truth, and the highest and only truth, so am I missing something?

Remember, a cone has two faces: one flat and one curved, which leads to the vertex or the apex. In scripture, we see that Jesus, the Son, and Jesus, the Holy Spirit, are in direct contact with the Father.

138

Get a piece of paper, and fold it to make a cone; do you notice that two ends come together making a point? That is the Son and the Holy Spirit working together with the Father. How does this apply to us?

John 16:13
But when he, the Spirit of truth, comes, he will guide you into all the truth. He will not speak on his own; he will speak only what he hears, and he will tell you what is yet to come.

The day we accepted Jesus as our Lord and Savior, we received the "cone of truth," and He will declare to us things that are to come. There is no need to go searching; this "cone of truth" is a one-stop-shop; it has everything. You will not lose your way, for He is the way. You will not believe or live a lie because He is truth, neither will you worry about being in darkness, for He is the light: the Light of life and the Light of the world. When you have the "cone of truth," you will be filled with everything sweet, for He said, *"How sweet are your words to my taste, sweeter than honey to my mouth!"* (Psalm 119:103). You are the salt of the earth: *"You are the salt of the earth. But if the salt loses its saltiness, how can it be made salty again? It is no longer good for anything, except to be thrown out and trampled underfoot." (Matthew 5:13).*

There are many who are turning away and will turn their ears from the "cone of truth" to myths, but you must remain in the truth and let the truth remain in you. There are many truths out there, but Jesus is the Absolute Truth.

Day 65
Flee Spiritual Pride

We ought to be careful of spiritual pride. I spent a whole week digesting Deuteronomy 9, and my self-examination mood was activated. Be careful not to think that God brought us out of any situation because of our righteousness.

God does not give us anything good or deliver us because of us. Whatever He does is to fulfill His Word, which He has declared from the beginning. He knows we are stiff-necked and rebellious, and if it had not been for Jesus, our mediator, we would have been destroyed.

I have so many instances where the Lord was quick to deliver me, not because I had uprightness of heart, but because it is not His will for me to perish. Instead of showing gratitude to God, I began to boast in my own filthy, so-called righteousness. There is also the tendency to think God acts on my behalf because He is supposed to and because I say I am serving Him. Scripture quickly corrected my arrogance in James 4:6: *"But he gives us more grace. That is why Scripture says: "God opposes the proud but shows favor to the humble.""*

Many times, the intercession of others reached out to God on my behalf. He has already given His promises concerning me, so He honors His Word.

Isaiah 55:11
So is my word that goes out from my mouth: it will not return to me empty but will accomplish what I desire and achieve the purpose for which I sent it.

Let us humble ourselves under the mighty hands of God. Put away selfish, spiritual pride, for in doing so, we will not anger the Lord. We were already children of wrath, but the saving power of His Son, Jesus Christ, redeems us. Let us show attitudes of gratitude whenever He chooses to deliver us and not boast in our filthy rags of righteousness.

Day 66
God Is Always Prepared To Clean Us

After giving Hannah her bath one morning, I was about to finish dressing her when she made a mess. What did I do? I changed her and cleaned her again.

Sometimes when the Lord cleans us up, by the time He gets us dressed, we mess up again. We did not stay clean for a minute, but God does not hesitate to clean us again, no matter how many times we mess up or how close our mess is to each other. God takes pleasure in seeing us clean and smelling fresh.

1 John 1:9
If we confess our sins, he is faithful and just and will forgive us our sins and purify us from all unrighteousness.

However, let us not take His mercies for granted. Our infant stage is slowly fading, and it is potty-training time and from potty-training to using the facilities by ourselves.

What stage are you? Are you pooping on yourself? Infant stage or potty training? Can you use the facility without supervision? Whichever stage you are, God is still standing by to clean you up.

Prayer:
Dear Lord, I messed up, but I am thankful that You are not a God who scorns Your children. I appreciate Your cleansing and endeavor to walk therein, in Jesus name. Amen.

Day 67
Spiritual Chafing

What is chafing? Chafing is a common skin problem caused by a combination of friction, moisture, and irritating fabric. Prolonged rubbing on the skin makes your skin sting or burn, and you develop a mild, red rash. In severe cases, chafing will include swelling, bleeding, or crusting.

It is always heart-rending whenever I must nurse the chafed bottom of my baby girl, but for her bottom to heal, I must clean in and around the affected area. I am familiar with the pain, as I have experienced chafing as well. It burns, itches, and it is uncomfortable.

I remembered when I was going through some spiritual and social chafing, and God decided to clean me up. From my screams and utter discomfort, He could not leave me in that state, or it would have resulted in a more serious outcome. As He cleaned my affected area, I agonized as He began the healing process. As I began to heal, I now had to make sure that the covering of the most delicate area of my body: the heart and mind, was always clean through the application of the Word of God, or it would result in another episode of chafing.

Like my baby's chafing, it was not always the covering that needed changing, but it can result from what was happening in her body, like teething, which results in her pooping. So it was with me; what was happening on the inside resulted in my painful chafing. Remember, it is what comes from the inside that defiles a man. The things that were coming from my heart and mind wounded me and created an itch and a burn like no other, so the Lord heard my cries and came to my rescue. Like a loving mother would, my Daddy Jesus cleaned me up and applied His blood so that I could be healed.

Whenever you experience chafing, spiritual or social, your cries will get God's attention. He will respond, and He will begin the cleaning process, which leads to healing. When that is done, ensure that you keep the area clean by being blameless; confessing every wrong to Him and let the mind of Christ be in you so your heart can be led by Him, so as not to break out into chafing again.

Day 68
True Happiness Comes From God

There is a difference between living in happiness and living in joy. Happiness depends on the state I am in and the circumstances surrounding that particular emotional state. Joy is a part of the fruit of the Spirit that He has graciously added to my life.

This joy I have comes from me believing in the Holy Ghost and Him filling me with peace and hope in the eternal. I must confess that there were years I had no joy, and all I had was an occasional episode of happiness. During those years, I struggled to find myself; I depended on external physical attention and events to make me happy. But after it was over, I went back to the same old person.

In doing so, I overworked myself to get things, go places and be among people I thought contributed to my happiness, without knowing that they sought the same joy I wanted but was looking in the wrong places and looking for it in the wrong things.

Psalm 37:4
Take delight in the Lord, and he will give you the desires of your heart.

Things changed when I had no choice but to look to God, who is the giver of true happiness and joy. The moment I started believing in His Word, I gradually started experiencing what it means to have joy. It no longer depended on the state I was in because I started to operate on Scripture, learning that whatever situation I am in to be content. Living joyfully is living in contentment.

Fast forward to today, I still have unpleasant circumstances and emotional breakdowns, but that does not take away the joy I have or the benefits it offers; neither does it take away from me infecting others with this same joy.

The joy the Lord gives is comparable to none. His joy brings about happiness. Our external circumstances should not dampen the joy we have because we receive it the moment we believe in Jesus Christ, and it is a part of the fruit of the Spirit that is essential in our wellbeing.

Day 69
Cancel The Devil's Access Key

Matthew 15:17-19
Don't you see that whatever enters the mouth goes into the
stomach and then out of the body? But the things that come out
of a person's mouth come from the heart, and these defile them.
For out of the heart come evil thoughts—murder, adultery,
sexual immorality, theft, false testimony, slander.

I remember smiling within myself and saying, "God, thank You because whenever I seem to be going off track, Your Word is loud in my head." Not long after the smile, I had a brief regression on some things, and because of the thoughts that began to generate, God had to confront me. But even before I was confronted with His Word, I really laughed this time, as I said, "Yes, satan, you not bringing me back there."

The devil knows what buttons to push. He knows my reaction to certain things; he knows my old way of responding, so he comes with his same old same old, but thank God. God blocked it! The devil worked on old information that he had in his docket about me; he knew that times gone by I would verbalize my thoughts, and that is how he plunged me into his web of defilement.

What he did not know was that while he was stockpiling my failures and shortcomings, Jesus, my Mediator, had another file that he knew nothing about, so when he pushed the button for those irritants in me, the button did not work, and nothing was spraying out. I feel a laugh coming on; this is too sweet. It felt like when your perfume has finished, and you are trying to get a little more from it, and nothing is left.

Take back your access key from the devil. Cancel his pass to come in and push any buttons; he has gained too long of an employment and has learned the ways of your organization (your heart)—terminate his contract. The CEO of your heart wants to make a new file and put you in a better position. Listen to the Holy Spirit within you, and let that which is holy, pure, edifying, and worthy of praise come from your mouth.

Knock, knock. Who's there? Defilement! Defilement who?

Day 70
He's An On-Time God

One evening, the Lord used a scenario to speak to my heart. I know it will speak to you too. As I was preparing dinner, the gas ran out. I told my husband the gas was finished. He called the gas man and asked him to deliver a cylinder of gas; then he left for other business and church. That was sometime after 6 PM. I sat and waited for the gas, but no delivery. So, I called my husband and told him I had not gotten the delivery. He said the gas man told him he was coming. I called the gas man myself and was told the same thing, so I sat down and waited.

Over one hour later, still no delivery. I called him again. He said, "I am coming. I made some other deliveries on my way from town. I am just five minutes away." So, I sat down and waited. Shortly after, I saw him and got my delivery.

What did I get from this?

2 Peter 3:8-9
But do not forget this one thing, dear friends: With the Lord a day is like a thousand years, and a thousand years are like a day. The Lord is not slow in keeping his promise, as some understand slowness. Instead he is patient with you, not wanting anyone to perish, but everyone to come to repentance.

In the middle of my daily walk and preparation to meet God, I am going to fail; my gas to continue the journey is going to burn out, and I am going to need a refill. I am going to call on the supplier, Jesus. He is going to respond, and He is saying to me, "I am on My way," but because of my impatience, I am going to keep calling for an answer when I have already gotten it, and all I have to do is sit and wait until He arrives.

He is God, and He knows what time He is going to stop by. He knows if I had received the gas in the usual quick time, I would not get the chance to finish cooking because the baby was being fussy, and I had to be nursing and cuddling her. He knows when my cry for help is immediate, and when I can wait a little longer. In waiting, I am developing the fruit of the Spirit: patience. When Hannah went to sleep, I did everything without being distracted by a cry or a fuss. God knew how He would have worked things out.

Stop calling and frustrating yourself. He heard you the first time. He has responded, but our impatience is getting the better of us. There is no need for Him to tell us He is making other deliveries. What we need to do is trust His Word and His answers to us. His timing is perfect! He knows that if He delivers at the time we ask, it will not be used right away because we have some things we need to put away first; things that will hinder us from finishing and finishing well. The songwriter said that He may not come when we want Him, but He will be there right on time.

God is an on-time God.

Day 71
Live For Jesus, Even If It Kills You

For three-quarters of my existence, I have been following Jesus Christ as Lord and Savior of my life. From the time I understood little about what I was doing until now, I am still learning the ways of Jesus.

I am going nowhere; backsliding is not an option anymore and the more years added to my life, the longer years of service I will have to live for Him. So, I thought, "Kefira, just live a good Christian life. You have gone through too much, seen too much, encouraged too much, led too many to Christ to just play church." I may as well live for Jesus completely and wholeheartedly. His return is right around the corner anyway. Romans 14:8 sums it up for me: *"If we live, we live for the Lord; and if we die, we die for the Lord. So, whether we live or die, we belong to the Lord."*

The moment a decision has been made to live Godly, our enemy, the adversary, the devil, is going to try and get us to live loose and ineffective lives as Christians. He is not interested in us backsliding; all he wants us to do is sidetrack every instruction from the Bible and give a carbon-copy of the real thing.

If you look around, you will notice that 2 Timothy 4:4 is happening: *"They will turn their ears away from the truth and turn aside to myths."* People are searching for what their itching ears want to hear, and so many times, what is said has no bearing on the Word of God. With God, if we break one of His commandments, we break all because all co-exist.

Live for Jesus, even if it kills you. Live for Jesus because He died for you. Live for Jesus because we are His only representative, and if the world does not know Him, it is because we have not been demonstrating what it is to know Jesus.

Now that we have discovered that backsliding does not make sense, neither is wayward living, level up. Live a good and impactful Christian life.

Day 72
Anticipate Your Tomorrow!

His hands are not short
      That He cannot reach to you
His eyes are never blind
    that He cannot see your tears
His ears are not deaf
      That He cannot hear you cry
Your tomorrow must be greater than today
Your tomorrow must be greater than today

No matter what I face
No matter what I see
No matter what comes my way
No matter how I cry
One thing I know
That is definitely in my heart
My tomorrow must be greater than today
My tomorrow must be greater than today (David Ekene)

After the choir sang, and it was time for "Moments behind the veil" worship, I could not help myself as the tears ran down my face. The Lord reassured me that my tomorrow would be greater than today. As I stood behind the pulpit, I began to speak into the atmosphere. It was the first I ever said openly to the congregation that I was one who cried a lot, among other things, just to be transparent. As I encouraged others, I received the encouragement myself, which opened up the atmosphere as people bowed in worship, and we adored Him for who He is and the assurance He sent our way. After church, I felt so whimsical. I am smiling even as I write.

We may cry now, but our tomorrow will be greater than today. We are hurting now, but our tomorrow will be greater than today. We are fighting the good fight now, not knowing when our fight will end, but our tomorrow will be greater than today. You are in an awkward position now, but your tomorrow will be greater than today. Whatever you are faced with today, whether bills, limitations, or discouragement, your tomorrow will be greater than today. Your tomorrow may be next year, week, month, or literally tomorrow. God always keeps His promises, and He never fails.

Day 73
No Beauty In Hostility

E phesians is a book I love, and every time I read it, I get something new or something I had overlooked jumps out at me.

In Ephesians 2:4-5, Paul reminds us that, "…because of his great love for us, God, who is rich in mercy, made us alive with Christ even when we were dead in transgressions—it is by grace you have been saved. "

I am no better than you because we have all been saved by grace through faith in our Lord Jesus Christ. These next verses really got me:

Ephesians 2:14-18
For he himself is our peace, who has made the two groups one and has destroyed the barrier, the dividing wall of hostility, by setting aside in his flesh the law with its commands and regulations. His purpose was to create in himself one new humanity out of the two, thus making peace, and in one body to reconcile both of them to God through the cross, by which he put to death their hostility. He came and preached peace to you who were far away and peace to those who were near. For through him we both have access to the Father by one Spirit.

If Jesus, who is our peace, has broken down the walls of separation so we can all have access by one Spirit to the Father, why is there so much segregation? Are we not connected by the same Spirit by which we have redemption? I am familiar with the thoughts we may occasionally use to justify why connections are not felt. If I am living a Christ-centered life, then I have access to the same Spirit as all believers. There must be a connection because it is the same source.

Ephesians 2:19-21
Consequently, you are no longer foreigners and strangers, but fellow citizens with God's people and also members of his household, built on the foundation of the apostles and prophets, with Christ Jesus himself as the chief cornerstone. In him the whole building is joined together and rises to become a holy temple in the Lord.

This is where the heart of the matter lies. I see where Scripture is being fulfilled before my very eyes and in the body of Christ to which the Lord has called us. Jesus Christ, the cornerstone, has canceled the stigma of being strangers and foreigners and has crossed us over to being citizens with the saints and members of the household of God. If we are being built together for a dwelling place of God in the Spirit, why is there so much tension and provocation in the body of Christ by the ones who are of the same Spirit? Or are they?

God delivered us from the same thing—being strangers and aliens—we practice with each other because some are of the view that they are on a different journey than that which the

Lord has laid out before the foundation of the earth. God had a plan, and He sent His Son to lay the foundation for the plan so that we can carry on the work to its completion. If we bite and devour one another, and if I think that my work is more significant than yours and is of more significance, it will not be completed. God has stated that if people (us) do not rise up, He will use stones to praise His name (See Luke 19:40).

Why do I boast, if not in the cross? Jesus destroyed the hostile, spiritual barrier between Jews and Gentiles, so why is there hostility between Gentiles? If I am saved by God's grace and you are saved by God's grace, it therefore means we are all His workmanship, created by Him for the purpose of good works.

I ask the Lord daily to walk with me so I may not fulfill the lust of the flesh. I am not talking about romance, but me wanting to practice and do things that are not fruitful, as the Scripture highlights:

Ephesians 4:31
Get rid of all bitterness, rage and anger, brawling and slander, along with every form of malice.

My daily cry and prayer is that I will be a vessel that the Spirit of God can reside in.

It is sad that demons unite for the tearing down and destroying of God's people, while we, as a body to which we are called, are doing the same. Our differences make us unique. Let us destroy hostility so restoration can take place, so we can continue to be built for the dwelling place of God in the Spirit.

Day 74
But: The Breakthrough Stopper

TRUST is a word that carries a lot of weight, more so, "trusting God." I have been having some inner conversations with the Lord as it relates to trusting Him. It is all good to say the words, "I trust You, Lord," because it sounds nice when it is rolling off my tongue, but it is the action that indicates whether or not I am mouthing off.

I have been told countless times to "Trust God." I even tell others the same. In my frequent conversations with God, I heard Him say, "You cannot trust Me and have a "but." I have researched this conjunction and realized that it is used to indicate the impossibility of anything other than what is stated. If I am going to trust God, I must do it wholeheartedly.

Proverbs 3:5-6
Trust in the Lord with all your heart and lean not on your own understanding; in all your ways submit to him, and he will make your paths straight.

The inconsistency of my human capacity has detoured me from the path God has directed, many times, based on my own understanding and being wise in my own eyes. Further dialogue would have God reminding me that "but" brings about doubts, and if I doubt Him, I will not get my breakthroughs or any other thing. The Lord taught me that He does not work with alternatives; I will either trust Him or not; no middle ground. I trust God, but He will not do everything for me.

I have gone ahead and done things He did not ordain. I was a very independent person who worked for everything I wanted. When the decision was made to resign from my job and do full-time ministry with my husband, I "but" God a lot. He told me that He would supply all my needs if I only trust and obey Him. With the many attempts to find a job, I should have realized that He had a different pathway for me. I had this long, buried passion for writing, but I decided that I would need money to fund it to accomplish this dream and birth this ministry. I sent out forty-five applications, with no response. Why did I waver concerning His promises to me? He did say He would supply my needs, so why did I think I could help God? I must believe that if He said He knows and has already made provisions to make it happen, then I need to just leave it at that.

My mind went back to the children of Israel and the many times God delivered them. Yet, they doubted God to the point of making a golden calf to lead them. The thought came as I was writing that if I cannot trust God, then I am in a phony relationship: just going through the motions, copying another person's saying and doing the opposite. Trusting is moving from the ground floor to the penthouse, but I find myself in the lobby at times, afraid of the other floors, which takes more courage, and more climb.

The conjunction "but" is a blessing stopper, deliverance blocker, healing hinderer, and truth deceiver. God's Word is yes and amen. His decisions concerning you cannot be spoilt with a "but." His possibilities are endless, and we cannot wear out the infinity of His existence. Our duty is to trust Him, as He says, and obey Him. When that is done, He will do His part.

Hope thou in God.

Day 75
Closet Cleaning (The Inner Man)

I had a feeling one evening, and not knowing what to make of it, I went into my room and cleaned out my closet. As I cleaned, I talked with myself concerning the shoes that were there; different sizes, colors, and smells, some totally ruined while some had a little more wear in them, but because of how long they were there uncleaned, they were not wearable.

As I swept through the places they had been, I heard the Lord speaking to me. Just like my closet, I had things inside me that needed cleaning out; things of different sizes that were completely ruining my life and were not profitable to my being. There were potentials in me that could have been more developed and should be, but because of how long I had put them down, they had gone dormant or rather dead, so they needed to be re-activated and some totally eliminated from my life.

I continued to sweep and pick out the good shoes while God was showing me that He was also cleaning out the things in me that were not good. They were ruined, and no wear was left in them. He told me I had things in me that did not belong to me, and they were affecting me and weighing me down. I had taken them on to myself, and it allowed me to change course and become angry. His Word was no longer what I relied on for answers. What He took out of me was even heavier than the bag of shoes. I became nervous and jittery, looking in awe at the things I was seeing and hearing.

When I was finished, I reorganized my closet after sweeping it clean. It smelled fresher, looked better, and my room felt cleaner. I opened it; I closed it repeatedly, looking at how different it was. God said to me, "You need to identify the things inside you that are of no use to you. Take them out. Clean the space and reorganize yourself." I was ashamed as He spoke to me. He reminded me of Hebrews 12:6-8: *"Because the Lord disciplines the one he loves, and he chastens everyone he accepts as his son." Endure hardship as discipline; God is treating you as his children. For what children are not disciplined by their father? If you are not disciplined—and everyone undergoes discipline—then you are not legitimate, not true sons and daughters at all."*

Have you checked the closet of your inner man lately? Are there any ruined items there that are not beneficial to you? Are there any that do not belong to you, but you hold them there for keepsake?

1 John 1:9
If we confess our sins, he is faithful and just and will forgive us our sins and purify us from all unrighteousness.

Do a cleaning. Get rid of the hoarding: bad spirits, envy, jealousy, malicious intent, bitterness, just to name a few. When the cleaning is completed, you will be left refreshed, compliments of our Father.

With every encounter we have with God, He is giving a message of rebuke, warning, affirmation, or consolation. Whichever situation we find ourselves in, we should be happy God still speaks to us.

~ Kefira Reid

Day 76
God Rewards Faithfulness!

2 Chronicles 16:9
For the eyes of the Lord range throughout the earth to strengthen those whose hearts are fully committed to him. You have done a foolish thing, and from now on you will be at war.

Proverbs 28:20
A faithful person will be richly blessed, but one eager to get rich will not go unpunished.

My family and I are proof that God rewards faithfulness. One day our washing machine shut down, and I had to wash by hand. I got so tired. I had to get up early in the mornings before the piercing sun. My hands got blisters and burns from the detergent; they were so tender; it was even difficult to shower after. There were so many clothes, yet I had to be out for church duties. Sometimes when I looked at the growing mountain of clothing, I was tempted to stay at home and just do laundry.

I felt so burdened and depressed, and I began to tell God about my feelings. I closed the doors to avoid seeing the pile of dirty clothes. Just before I went to church, somebody brought us a brand-new machine. We were planning to go down to our sister's house to do laundry after church, but God blessed us with a new machine and some money to get food as we had nothing to eat after church.

If you are in a difficult situation and cannot see your way out, do not think about the other options or what others are doing. Continue serving God diligently and wholeheartedly. If you remain faithful to Him, He will remain faithful to you. God cannot lie. Even if we become unfaithful, He still remains faithful. Whatever you do, do it as unto the Lord and not unto men (See Colossians 3:23). God rewards faithfulness.

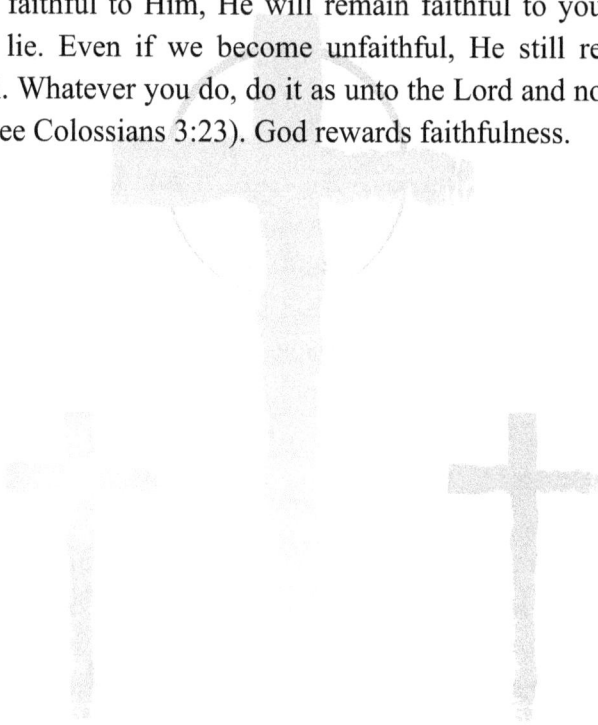

Day 77
Cut The Stink From Your Tongue!

1 Peter 2:1
Therefore, rid yourselves of all malice and all deceit, hypocrisy, envy, and slander of every kind.

I saw a post that read, "Never trust your tongue when your heart is bitter and broken; hush until you are healed." I can relate. In my brokenness, I have spoken things that could not be further from the truth. I have made some declarations that I wished I had not made, and today I am paying the consequences of the words spoken. Jesus said it is not what we eat that defiles us but that which comes from our mouth (See Matthew 15:11), so I had to reap the results of my words.

It is a good thing that He is a God of chances, and He does not always deal with me according to what my ways deserve; else I would have fallen victim by my own tongue countless times. At times, the words spoken hurt others in the desperation of the situation, and words catch on easily.

Sometimes, because of how you feel, your tongue causes you to pull others in situations they do not belong. Utterances are made that you know are not so, and it is a struggle to recover. The fire was lit and has spread like wildfire. In Esther's story, a decree was made to kill all Jews, and it could not be reversed, but another decree was written for them to fight back. You have made declarations that may be irreversible, but you can make another one that can counteract and override them.

Philippians 4:8
Finally, brothers and sisters, whatever is true, whatever is noble, whatever is right, whatever is pure, whatever is lovely, whatever is admirable—if anything is excellent or praiseworthy—think about such things.

If we practice thinking right, then the tongue can only speak things worthy of praise.

Day 78
Not Going Back

There is a song that says, "I won't go back, I can't go back, to the way it used to be, before Your presence came and change me." This is a declaration that needs to be repeated so the reality can be lived.

Saying, "I will not go back" is not as easy as it sounds, providing that the circumstances surrounding not going back has intensified, and the options are few. We err so often. His presence is always changing us. We can easily say the words, but sometimes putting the spoken into action is not done.

Going over the experiences in life, I discovered that the real issue is not the problem at hand, but what the problem has left on the inside: the emotional hurt, betrayal, rejection, feelings of not being good enough, and the numbness that it brings. For example, the death of a loved one. We cry over it, but then the reality of it hits when you remember that the person is no longer around. Feelings start to generate, the loneliness, emptiness, and a whole lot more depressing feelings.

Philippians 3:13-14 says:
Brothers and sisters, I do not consider myself yet to have taken hold of it. But one thing I do: Forgetting what is behind and straining toward what is ahead, I press on toward the goal to

win the prize for which God has called me heavenward in Christ Jesus.

Living our reality of not going back is acknowledging that there is something behind us that is not a lesson worth repeating. What is it that we are saying we will not go back to? Is it our reality? Burying whatever it is that we are not going back to with false progression will only result in us going back because it was not dealt with. We can say we have, but our actions are going to tell a different story.

Matthew 11:28-29
Come to me, all you who are weary and burdened, and I will give you rest. Take my yoke upon you and learn from me, for I am gentle and humble in heart, and you will find rest for your souls.

May you be released into the rest of Him who loves us.

Day 79
Something Happens When We Call On The Name Of Jesus

Have you ever been in a situation where you want Jesus' immediate attention, but because of where you are at the time and circumstances surrounding the situation, you have to whisper His name? You did it with so much passion and contrition that Jesus had to respond.

Romans 10:13
For, "Everyone who calls on the name of the Lord will be saved."

I have been in that very position. Every so often I am pushed in such a way that I must call on Jesus so that He can take immediate action concerning my heart and mind. I remember one instance when I wanted to call Jesus aloud, and I could not because my daughter was in my hand, and she had fought long and hard to finally fall asleep. I opened my mouth as wide and as hard as I could, and I bellowed the name, "JESUS." I did so three times. I was desperate for Him, and at that name, JESUS, the name which is above every other name, the matchless name, the name that demons trembled at, my heart and mind had to be subjected. I lay my daughter down, went to bed, and had the best two and a half hours of sleep I had ever had before she woke me up with a small cry.

There is no magnitude of a situation, time frame, place, or people that can stop you from calling on your Savior, Jesus. If you call Him softly, He hears it; loudly, He hears you; as long as your heart is broken and sincere about the matter, He will not despise, but respond accordingly because His will is not that any of us should perish.

Day 80
Valuing Others Better Than Ourselves

You have permission to outshine me because I have already applied Scripture to value others above myself. Did I want to or still want to? No, but allowing the Word of God to shape my life takes a lot of sacrifices that will affect the carnal nature that is fighting with the spiritual.

I have been hurt and abused by people so many times. I used to wonder how long it would take to heal. But God has been nursing my bruises. On my road to healing and Christ-like living, I find that the pieces of the puzzle must be re-shuffled so the right pieces can fit in the right spots if I am ever going to be a true believer God can use to reach the masses. Ephesians 4:32 encourages us to: *"Be kind and compassionate to one another, forgiving each other, just as in Christ God forgave you."*

We are all servants of Jesus, and every member of the body is useful. So, whichever part of the body of Christ you are, you have an important function because we are incomplete without you.

Day 81
Though Fragile, God Will Handle You With Care

I am FRAGILE. The very thing designed to help build me will sometimes break me. I am in a metamorphosis stage, and while I am destined to be a butterfly, my butterfly lifespan will take effect when I transition from this side of life into the better.

The cycle of change uproots and exposes a lot of things I did not know were hidden underneath. There were some ugly things, some nasty things, and some things that give off a stench. As I changed from one stage to the next, I realized that I was not as strong and well put together as I previously thought. But God has been my hope, Sovereign Lord, and confidence since my youth (See Psalm 71:5).

I have been a follower of the Way for an exceedingly long time, twenty-four years to be exact. I began my Christ-like living twelve years prior to writing this book. During those years, I utterly understood what it takes to be a Christian and how I should be living as a Christian. It has been an eye-opening discovery. I discovered things about myself I did not know existed; things that were of value and things that needed to be aborted. I also discovered some qualities that will be ready to deposit in others when given the chance and the time to develop. In all of these experiences, I took comfort in Psalm 121:3: *"He will not let your foot slip—he who watches over you will not slumber."*

In the transitioning years living the Christ-centered life, I had to endure what Jesus said I would as His follower. Boy, did it hurt! I had to throw away philosophies that were not in accordance with the Word of God. I had to disassociate myself from attitudes that were not in alignment with the path of Jesus. I did not have a lot of friends, but I had to step away from my association with the ones who continuously disregard the instructions of Jesus and seemingly stunted my growth.

The contents in your box may be fragile, but you have a God who will handle you with care. Your transitions may be painful, but the end results promise to be fulfilling.

Embrace the change!

Day 82
Chosen

2 Timothy 2:19
Nevertheless, God's solid foundation stands firm, sealed with this inscription: "The Lord knows those who are his," and, "Everyone who confesses the name of the Lord must turn away from wickedness."

As I browse through and inspect my life, I cannot help but ask God for His continued leadership so that I may be among the remnants. Matthew 22:1-14 gives us a clear example of those who are called the chosen. There is a call to the kingdom of God, and though many have come and will continue to come, it is only those who have accepted the call, dressed themselves for the call, and carry out the function of the call that will be accepted in the position as heirs and joint heirs with God.

I remember going to an interview. When I got there, a few others were already there. All of us were called for an interview because we met the criteria or seemingly had experience that could work to their advantage. In the batch of interviewees were various qualifications. Being the type of person I am, I began the socializing process. I engaged in conversations with those who may be prospective co-workers. I asked one of them if they had ever worked in a financial institution before. She said no, but she had worked as a supervisor and had various experiences working with people.

The employer already knows who they would select based on our experiences, qualifications, physical appearances, and interviews. From the batch of called applicants that were interviewed, they chose two persons, and I was not one of them. Upon investigation gathered by one of the applicants, I realized that I would not have been chosen given the contractual agreement. It would have been hard for me to meet the job requirements as I did not possess the ability to carry out the performance task. I knew I would not keep up.

The invitation that has been extended to all will not result in all being chosen, not because God did not choose us, but by our own choice to not come in agreement with His criteria of being a part of the chosen. While we may be chosen, we must still maintain the status of the chosen by the way we reflect the master Chooser; our lives should represent Him.

There are several persons whom we have given to the Lord, who are not a part of His remnant. In fact, there are some persons who are not yet saved but by virtue of their future decision will thrust them into the ownership of God; they are sometimes condemned and written off as doomed, but God knows they are candidates for heaven. We may have a church of three hundred, but only a handful may be chosen. God knows our future: He also knows those who will stay and suffer with Him, follow Him, and walk with Him all the way. God is not biased. He gave us the capacity to choose, and we can either choose to be His or remain among the called. Peter told us to work hard to make our calling and election sure (See 2 Peter 1:10).

Day 83
God Doesn't Say Oops

One morning I was browsing through the news channels that I subscribed to, and there was one piece that caught my attention. I had to share it with my husband. It made me chuckle too.

The headlines read: "British airways apologies to travelers after flight lands 525 miles away from destination." I laughed, even though it was a serious matter. We trust humans with our lives when they sometimes cannot even remember what destination to take us, but cannot trust God. My God has never forgotten or made a mistake in bringing me to my appointed destination. He will never apologize for sending me or taking me anywhere. He knows exactly where my next stop is, and even if there is a detour, He already orchestrated it, and it is not a surprise to Him.

Psalm 33:13-15
From heaven the Lord looks down and sees all mankind; from his dwelling place he watches all who live on earth— he who forms the hearts of all, who considers everything they do.

God is in a class all by Himself. He has no earthly classification given to Him by man. He does not have 20/20 vision; He is all-seeing, all-knowing, all-hearing; He is everything. He never says "oops" to any situation. He is the Inventor of the inventor, who invents the situations. TRUST HIM.

Day 84
Unprofitable Conversations

S hun the temptation for wanting to tit for tat; it only reduces your steps in climbing the ladder of being free and stunts your growth of becoming a matured and wise human being. It sometimes seems fitting to make a comeback, especially when you think your comeback is better but, like our pattern Jesus, He was oppressed and treated harshly, yet He never said a word. He was led like a lamb to the slaughter.

Isaiah 53:7
He was oppressed and afflicted, yet he did not open his mouth; he was led like a lamb to the slaughter, and as a sheep before its shearers is silent, so he did not open his mouth.

Some of the practices that have worked for me are being blind, deaf, and dumb to some things. The less I see, hear, and know, the better I am.

1 Corinthians 13:4-5
Love is patient, love is kind. It does not envy, it does not boast, it is not proud. It does not dishonor others, it is not self-seeking, it is not easily angered, it keeps no record of wrongs.

Sometimes we claim we love, yet all the negative aspects of love spoken of in the above Scripture is being practiced; it is not the Word of God that is in error but us. I have learned not to point fingers at others but to see the error in me. If Scripture outlines what love is and I am doing the opposite, there is no justification for my doings but to turn from my erring ways.

It is not time to camouflage light, but to be the light.

If God points us to it, He wants us to change it or be it.

~ Kefira Reid

Day 85
Give God Your Frustrations

I remember taking out my hair extensions. It was a long time coming. My own hair was flaked and dirty; I could literally feel the dirt on my scalp. While cutting the thread, I accidentally cut my hair. I looked in disbelief and proceeded to get the other extensions out. I struggled as I searched for the threads that looked so much like my hair, making sure not to cut any more.

I managed to cut through. When I was almost finished, my frustration became elevated. I became so impatient that I thought of just cutting my own hair to get rid of it all. The hair got entangled in the threads, and I could not find any part to clip. I was becoming hot and tormented with the bits and pieces of hair falling on my skin, coupled with the flakes, and that pushed my frustrations to the limit. I took a walk to get some fresh air, then went back to it. Finally, a breakthrough; they were all out.

I went to the pipe, took a bow, and shampooed away. It was a relief when the water hit my head, and I started scrubbing. There it was: the freshness; the clean scalp feeling, and looking healthy. My head felt lighter, my face looked brighter, and my pimples disappeared.

2 Corinthians 12:9
But he said to me, "My grace is sufficient for you, for my power is made perfect in weakness." Therefore I will boast all the more gladly about my weaknesses, so that Christ's power may rest on me.

The thing you are trying to get out of is elevating your frustrations; you try to handle it by yourself, but you end up cutting the wrong link, the wrong people. You can feel the dirt, heat, and flake from happenings that are falling on you, and you feel like just giving up. Do not give up. Take a walk, breathe in the fresh air; breakthrough is right there. Find your pipe—Jesus. Take a wash, feel the cleanness, and smell the freshness as your space becomes lighter, your face brighter, and that hard to handle situation disappears.

Day 86
Friendship Evangelism

Jesus did not come for the saved, but for the unsaved, so He spent His days after the synagogue meeting with those who needed Him.

In evaluating those I had been in association with, I realized they were not saved. My husband told me that I did "friendship evangelism," and then I realized that my previous friendship with my now "bestie" was because of that same thing: FRIENDSHIP EVANGELISM.

Matthew 9:10-17 is an example of how Jesus demonstrated this friendship evangelism. From my experience, what it did not take was a lot of talking and trying to convince her to get saved. Like Jesus, it had a lot to do with my lifestyle. We did most things together: movies, trips, work, and otherwise. We shared the same room at every work-related event; we often got dressed and took ourselves out, so she got a chance to see me demonstrating what it means to be a follower of Christ.

It took her six years to come into a relationship with Jesus. Now she is rooted and grounded in Christ. She is not perfect, but she has learned what it is to be blameless, and being blameless is not sinless but ensuring there is no unconfessed sin before God, our Father.

186

Our lives should be affecting the unsaved. Instead, there is so much competition among Christians trying to prove themselves as more in right standing with God than the other, yet the Bible clearly states that our righteousness is as filthy rags.

Instead of trying to prove ourselves to each other, let us be what God has called us to be and do: make disciples. There is no need for you to take them on by the dozen, but one friendship at a time will aid in winning the lost for the kingdom. Start today in evangelizing, and what better way to start than through friendship evangelism.

Day 87
Choices

I am on a daily quest to learn to make choices that will lead me to being a Christ-like individual. In the center of it, I am having hiccups. I consider these hiccups necessary because even though they seem unpleasant, they humble me and allow me to see myself as a sinner saved by God's grace.

While growing up, I was constantly hearing the phrase: "Your choices can either make you or break you." I have made choices that broke me and some that made me. After I had my son, Jehiel, I said I wanted a baby girl. I made the choice to get pregnant, even though I was not in control of the results. I had another boy. I was disappointed and decided not to try for another, even though my husband wanted a daughter.

After four years, I got a word that God was giving me all that was on my list; I knew my list had a daughter on it. I shrugged in sarcasm because I thought it was not going to happen. I already made it up in my mind not to find out if it would be so. Even when the Lord told me in a dream, I was still reluctant. I did not get my daughter until I made the choice to explore the possibility; hence, the result.

God gave choices, and even though He promises me things, it is not until I activate the choice to be obedient that results are forthcoming. I find that denying myself daily is not something I am doing in totality as I find solace in gratifying the self. The choice to be selfless, gentle, and to love as He loves are attributes of Christ that I am aiming to be like.

I read a quotation from Anne Ortlund that says: *"Whatever God asks you to be, He enables you to be."* Ephesians 1:3 tells us that we are blessed with all spiritual blessings in heavenly places, which is an indication that we are more than able to make choices that reflect Jesus Christ.

I am willing to make the choices that will highlight the possibilities of being Jesus' reflection and avoid making choices that will have a negative impact on my being. Today, I choose to be honest with myself, acknowledge that I am not self-sufficient, and verbally tell God that I need Him. I need Him to fix me so I can be of use to Him.

Choices are road maps in fulfilling our destiny. The choice to live Christ-like already seals the deal of our eternal destination. We may have already made some bad decisions, but life means you can correct them.

Whatever we gain, whatever we have experienced and is experiencing, is as a result of our choices.

~ *Kefira Reid*

Day 88
Be Honest In Your Progression

Sometimes we make promises to ourselves, and we end up breaking them. I do not think I have reached the place that I had my goal set on; it feels like wounds are being opened; wounds that I thought were healed, and it hurts a lot. I said I would not allow myself to get back to that place, and I do not know how I got there again. I guess I never realized how deeply scarred I was. With others looking to me to be the example, I forgot to look after myself and take time to heal. Instead, I pushed myself so hard and overlooked the things that affected me, that the moment I thought of taking a breath of freshness, there they appeared again.

I crack, and I am bleeding. I have looked over things for so long that they are resurfacing. I do not want to just post Scriptures that has not been having any effect on me and pretend that I am fine. I want to know that when I say I am over a matter, I am. It is a new year, and I had all intentions to start fresh, but I did not realize that I did not write off the old accounts that were indebted to me. So, I had a balanced brought forward into this year, unknowingly. Only time alone can really bring back things buried.

I know me; the moment I find myself crying over things that had happened to me, I know I have not dealt with it. So, immediately I cried out to Jehovah Rapha, my Healer. I asked Him to heal my heart and fix me. I wanted to continue crying, but the tears suddenly dried up as I was reminded of Philippians 3:12-14: *"Not that I have already obtained all this, or have already arrived at my goal, but I press on to take hold of that for which Christ Jesus took hold of me. Brothers and sisters, I do not consider myself yet to have taken hold of it. But one thing I do: Forgetting what is behind and straining toward what is ahead, I press on toward the goal to win the prize for which God has called me heavenward in Christ Jesus."*

I knew God had done His part; I was left to make adjustments, so I had to share this experience.

Maybe, like me, you have some brought forwards on accounts indebted to you—those that should have been written off as bad debts—and there is a deficit in your new balance. You may have overlooked them in the event that you were trying to reach a settled account. You have an accountant who fixes and corrects every bad account; His name is Jesus. But first you must bring it to His attention, so when the auditor, the devil, comes, all accounts are settled, and he cannot accuse you of mismanagement or theft.

Cry, if you must, and hand it to Jesus. Do not feel ashamed that you have regressed; give it to Him and take time to properly work yourself into honest progression. I am sure He heard me, and He will hear you too.

Day 89
Don't Lose Heart!

The Lord took me through another period of testing to let you know we serve a God who specializes in things thought impossible. For those who are looking for answers from everywhere and in anything else other than the Creator of the universe, the One who spoke things into being, I want to let you know that God is real and He can be touched with the feelings of your infirmities (See Hebrews 4:15). Isaiah 41:10 proves to me that He will fight for us, and He will uphold us: *"So do not fear, for I am with you; do not be dismayed, for I am your God. I will strengthen you and help you; I will uphold you with my righteous right hand."*

Our beautiful daughter was admitted to the hospital one Saturday after we took her to the doctor to find out what was making her cry so uncontrollably. She was groaning and grunting in pain, and I became so weak in my bowels, I could not bear up. After the first abdominal x-ray was done, the doctor said it was unclear and mentioned intussusception, where the intestine invaginates into the adjoining intestinal lumen, causing bowel obstruction. I lost it immediately because it was the first I had heard that term and condition. A second x-ray was done, but there was no conclusive answer as to what was happening. Hannah was still crying and having occasional fevers. Her blood work was done and came back clean; no sign of dengue, and nothing wrong with the blood, but nothing beats prayer.

She was released Sunday evening with a referral to do an abdominal ultrasound, which we did, and it came back clean. Her organs were fine, and her gut was normal. The devil tried and had failed again. It was evident that from day one, he had to interfere with what God had established and ordained. It was no coincidence that she was born in the eighth month, and at eight months old, the devil was still trying to harm her. We are victorious, and our defense is in the Lord. He never said that the weapons would not form, He said they would not prosper.

When our baby came home, I went into celebratory mode. God had done it again, and I knew He had His hands on us, and all the promises that He gave to me, to us, as a family, He kept them and continues to keep them. I now wake up with the assurance of His security for me, knowing whatever storms He may take me through that I will not be blown away with the wind. I walk with the assurance that He orders my steps, and He knows the plot to the next chapter of my life and the life of my family. I have confidence in His Word, and I will walk tall and proud, knowing whatever He ordains, He has His perfect plan.

Are you faced with situations, and you cannot understand why they are happening to you? Are you getting tired of being tested and proven? Maybe you are saying, like me, that you do not want to be great; you just want a simple, normal life and live a good Christian life. God knows what you would be and what you would have been involved in, so He laid out the map of your life. Even if you detoured, He knew you would, and even in the detour, He still had that in His plans; nothing takes Him by surprise.

I was told that God makes tough soldiers through the hardest battles. He knows what vessels we are: honour or dishonor. You are heading to your best life now. Just do not lose heart.

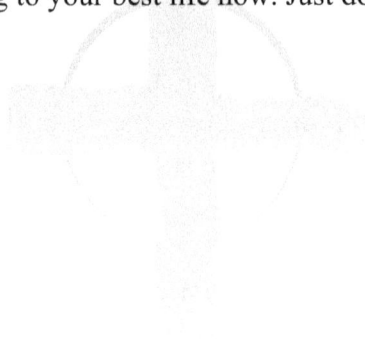

Day 90
Don't Compromise Who You Are

Romans 13:14
Rather, clothe yourselves with the Lord Jesus Christ, and do not think about how to gratify the desires of the flesh.

I have done a lot of good things; I got myself involved in some bad things, but the one thing I am proud of the most is how genuine I am. I do not mean to self-boast, but I have experienced some insincerities in my lifetime, and because I have encountered them, I have dedicated my life to become a real person, even in my hurt. I had to endure being used and abused socially and emotionally and still end up being the same person I was, even after the hurt.

When I think I have been wronged, I want to defend my honour. I want to retaliate; I want to hurt others who may have hurt me so badly, but to do it, I find it hard, and thinking about how, when, and where to do it sends an adrenaline rush inside me like no other. Sometimes I attempt the process but had to abort as I am reminded of Romans 12:19: *"Do not take revenge, my dear friends, but leave room for God's wrath, for it is written: "It is mine to avenge; I will repay," says the Lord."*

I have always lived with this concept that I become what I practice, so I make the best of the opportunity that presents itself to be the best version of who God has intended for me to be. I may be slow in getting it all together, but it is planted, and the seedling is about to become a tree that offers shade.

Do not compromise who you are to satisfy someone's inability to recognize real.

Day 91
Anxiety

Philippians 4:6
Do not be anxious about anything, but in every situation, by
prayer and petition, with thanksgiving, present your requests
to God.

A nxiety is a form of worrying and being uneasy about a certain outcome. Even though Scripture said I should not let my heart be troubled (See John 14:1), sometimes I can't help myself. I want to share with you how I have been dealing with anxiety, the highs and lows, and how it has affected my life.

For as long as I can remember, I have always been anxious. It has affected me from a child going into my teenage years, into adolescence, and then adulthood. I do not know if it is something that can be eliminated altogether. I worry about what to eat and drink and what to wear, even though God says not to (See Matthew 6:25). I worry about my kids and how they will turn out in the future. I worry about how they will manage in school. I worry about the church and if I am liked or loved and how I am affecting God's people, when all I should be doing is putting in the work and let God do the rest. I even worry about things that I do not have any business worrying about.

I remember doing four interviews, and I was so anxious that I became obsessed with my phone: checking emails and missed calls to see if I had received a callback or an email informing me of my acceptance. I read the Scripture but, at times, it is hard for me to apply what it says because I allow the magnitude of the situation to get the better of me. God has promised that He will perfect that which concerns me and give me an expected end (See Psalm 138:8). However, when I make comparisons with the other interviewees, I cannot help but wonder if I was qualified enough, knowledgeable enough, or even smart enough to get the job. In those dark times, I cannot process Scriptures like 2 Corinthians 9:8, which tells me that God is able to bless me abundantly in all things and at all times, so I have all that I need, and I will abound in every good work. Sometimes the easiest thing to do is worry.

I need to get the concept of not worrying right. There will arise situations that will cause me to worry. I am trying as best as possible to believe God like Abraham did. As I take a step away from anxiety, I am hopeful that that which He has for me will come at His appointed time.

It is not as easy, as some may put it, not to worry, but belief in God's Word is a start to experiencing the joys of not worrying. Let us take Him at His Word and see the wonders that unfold.

Day 92
Living In Harmony

The desire of God is for His children to live in harmony. The question I often ask myself is: "Whose child am I?" The good that I want to do, I do not, but when the detestable comes, I relish in it.

I am trying to live in the harmony that God requires, but I must resolve conflicts quickly with love for me to do that. The thing is, I do not know what the conflict is most of the time, and I have been at a place where I will love you irrespective of what happens, and though I search through and through, sometimes I am unable to identify the problem. I am also aware that I may even hurt someone without consciously knowing it. At times, the thing I consider to be nothing can be a big something to others.

Scripture tells me that when I go to the altar and remember that my brother has something against me, I should leave my gift at the altar and reconcile. Sometimes that is the hardest thing for me to do because I do not want to be the bigger or more matured person. When I know that I have tried to reach out but had gotten nowhere, I am left with no more options. I want to live Scripture and avoid drama. It is even harder for me when I know I had just dealt with something similar a season ago, and it keeps replicating itself.

Matthew 18:21-22

Then Peter came to Jesus and asked, "Lord, how many times shall I forgive my brother or sister who sins against me? Up to seven times?" Jesus answered, "I tell you, not seven times, but seventy-seven times."

In my place of questions and answers, I relate to you my experiences and how I am moving to a place of total transformation into Christ-like living. To date, I am not bitter or unforgiving; thank God for that. I am trying my best to live in harmony with my brethren. As I continue to grow in grace and in the knowledge of our Saviour, Jesus Christ, I desire to live Bible, so my living speaks for me.

In Philippians 4:2-7, Euodia and Syntyche are encouraged to replace their bitterness with gentleness and to live in peaceful harmony, rejoicing in the Lord. You may have fallen into conflict with your brother or sister or you may not know what the conflict is about, but one of the things that has helped me is praying for the person and their wellbeing. Do not pray unfavorable prayers; eventually, you will realize that the love of God in you extends from your heart, and you will start loving as He loves. If those you are in conflict with are God's children, then harmony will be an ingredient in the relationship.

Day 93
I Made It

This was my declaration at the beginning of 2019, "I made it. 2018 did not take me." I looked back to see how far I had come amidst the fiery darts, high waters, and dry seasons. My scars were evidence of what I had been through, but not what I am or will become.

I have had some bad years, but 2018 was my worst. It was a year of intense testing; it was the year I thought I would not survive the rapid attacks I encountered, and the year people decided they no longer needed to stick around. It was the year the enemy came hard against my family, finances, marriage, children, and the church. It was the year I cried the most. It was the year I had many unsuccessful job interviews. It was the year the devil tried to snatch my baby girl from the womb, but she made it. It was the year I spent my birthday in the hospital, making sure my Hannah-Amanda was okay. It was the year I got the most injections, and the year I visited the doctor the most. It was the year the enemy tried to set an ungodly pattern for me to follow: resentment, bitterness, hatred, unforgiveness, and regression, but I made it.

Amidst the worst, I got some good and best too. It is not over till it is over, and I am a testament to that saying. It was the year I experienced the love of God the most. Throughout all

201

the bad experiences mentioned above, His Word has proven true because it was that year that Scripture came alive in my life.

2 Corinthians 12:9
But he said to me, "My grace is sufficient for you, for my power is made perfect in weakness." Therefore I will boast all the more gladly about my weaknesses, so that Christ's power may rest on me.

I developed more patience, exercise more fruit of the Spirit, and my character was increasingly becoming that of Christ. I am not sure how many worst I have left because with the whining down to go home to glory, there will be increased trials and testing, disappointments, and frustration, but the same infinite and faithful God who brought me through 2018, will definitely guide me through the coming years.

The result of what we went through in 2018 is what brought us into each new year. We did not get an F. We may have gotten a grade IV or V, which meant there was a re-sit but may we capitalize on the lessons learned and proceed with our exams with confidence and the knowledge of the course so that we can come out with a grade 1.

May you have a God-filled and successful year.

Day 94
God Has Already Prepared And Approved It

God has His thoughts on you, so there is no need to feel inferior. God proves Himself repeatedly when He reaffirms and reveals His thoughts towards us.

Years ago, I started my degree in Banking and Finance but had some difficulties finishing. I tried every legal way possible to see how I could finish, but it became more difficult as I was denied job offers that I was interviewed for. It brought me to a place of reservation, feeling incomplete, so I started to shy away from the company of my peers or my colleagues in ministry because I thought I was not on their level.

Sometimes I was convinced I was brilliant with or without the paper that certified that someone has been schooled at a certain level, but there were just some moments when I felt out of it. But God! God, my Father, the Infinite One, went to London, England, and revealed His thoughts to someone concerning me; someone who knew nothing of my frustrations and what my greatest desires were. While I was thinking how much I would love to be complete and done, even if I did not get a job, I received a text on messenger. The text read: *"I had a dream last night. U graduated with your masters with honours. Mario n the others were cheering you on."* Those were his exact words.

God loves me and always has His thoughts on me.

Psalm 139:16-17
Your eyes saw my unformed body; all the days ordained for me
were written in your book before one of them came to be. How
precious to me are your thoughts, God! How vast is the sum of
them!

God is not a man that he should lie. If He said it, He will do it.
If He is going to do it, He has already made the preparations
and provisions to get it done. Do not worry about how, when,
or where; just trust Him. He has it covered.

Day 95
God Has Better

I remember doing many job interviews and getting no acceptance. I really needed a job. One of the associates who was called back for another interview sent me a text that she had received a call to review the contract for the acceptance of the job. I was happy for her. We were developing into what could become a good friendship. The problem was, I did not get any calls, and I was at my wit's end. I was frustrated and anxious at the same time, which plunged me into thinking I was not good enough. All my thoughts were centered on why I was not getting any calls. Was it because God had something better for me? Did I not impress them enough? I kept thinking that maybe I would get a call soon.

As the day progressed into evening, I was still checking emails and looking for calls or missed calls. That did not happen, but I was cheered up when I was taken to one of my favorite restaurants. I still believed that God would give me a suitable job in His timing. Until I am blessed with that suitable job, I rest comfortably in Philippians 4:19, *"And my God will meet all your needs according to the riches of his glory in Christ Jesus."*

Are you feeling disappointed that you did not get a callback? Maybe you wanted a promotion or a raise. Guess what, maybe

God has something better, or He is developing a little more patience in you. Whatever it is, His timing and choices are perfect.

Day 96
God Knows The Truth About You

One of the ministers who had a role in my development in Christendom often uses this phrase: "Truth crush to earth will someday rise again." Truth cannot be hidden, no matter how we try to hide it. It is like a leopard; its spots cannot be changed, even if it tries.

The Lord has been dealing with me in some kind of way, and I realize that though I may change lanes at times, I eventually get back to the original lane because both lanes lead to different destinations. I do not have to pretend to be who I am not. I have learned to give God my naked self so He can dress me in the most appropriate attire that best suits Him so that I can complement Him. Every now and again, I am reminded of Revelation 22:11: *"Let the one who does wrong continue to do wrong; let the vile person continue to be vile; let the one who does right continue to do right; and let the holy person continue to be holy."*

Do not allow your cry for attention to plunge you into a replica of someone else. If you are a loving person, be that. If you are a giving person, be that. Let your genuine attributes speak for you. Everyone will not love or appreciate you. When your truth is revealed, the right ones will recognize it. The important thing is: GOD, your Father, knows the truth about you.

Day 97
Look Out For The Button Pushers

L ook out for the button pushers who are intentional in their bid to make you act contrary to how you are supposed to.

I remember a time I was going out of my mind. If the Lord did not stop me in my tracks and blocked the plots of those working under the influence of the devil, I would have lost it big time. Being in ministry has had its fair share of struggling to do what is right and balance being rational or confrontational. I had instances where I felt like I would defend myself at all cost, but when I thought about it, I would only be lowering my standards and compromising my integrity. Sometimes the way I feel like expressing myself is not edifying to either me or the other persons involved. Romans 12:18 encourages us: *"If it is possible, as far as it depends on you, live at peace with everyone."*

Take my advice: even if you think about it and you want to express your feelings in a way satisfying to your liking, run away. You will experience the built-up rush of not responding, but you will be saved from the embarrassment and guilt later.

Day 98
You Are Not Inferior

When I am at my lowest, I hear God's voice the loudest.

I was reminiscing on what had been happening in and around me one day, and I began to look again at the people who I think were more worthy and more right than me. Immediately, I started feeling inferior. I started speculating and arriving at conclusions that could not be farther from the truth. I am sometimes of the view that I have done enough for God to not want, love, and use me anymore. I started looking at the people who had done so much for God and still ended up with their lives being disrupted, and I thought: if that could happen to such good persons, what about me, who is the least?

I kept replaying in my head the words of my brother: "Sis, God loves you." I have heard that phrase so many times with the very same tone and from so many ministers. I heard it when I was struggling as a teen in my hometown. God started to speak when I asked, "Why me when there are others better than me?"

He said, "Some stay with Me for what they can get and when times are good, but you stay regardless of what you get or what happens to you."

I knew then that I would be okay in spite of the turmoil around me. God really loves me, and I love it when He speaks to me; it feels fatherly and gives me this sense of security that Daddy is looking out for His princess.

Ephesians 2:10
For we are God's handiwork, created in Christ Jesus to do good works, which God prepared in advance for us to do.

Even if you think you are the least among others and are unqualified, your misfits fit right into the space God has where He can turn things around and in the direction you are destined to go.

You did not choose Him; He chose you and chose to love you. You are not inferior. Do not believe the lies of the devil. God has His thoughts on you.

Day 99
We All Have Our Place In The Kingdom

It is said that a healthy meal consist of all the food groups and vegetables, and fruits should incorporate all the colors as they represent something and contributes to the wellbeing of our bodies.

I may not be the main ingredient, but I am necessary for the taste of the meal. I may be a sweet pepper; maybe you are a garlic, while another is a purple or white onion; each gives the meal a superb taste, and as much as the onion may affect the eyes and give an aftertaste, our meat is not enjoyable without the onion and garlic. Some ingredients are added at a later part in the cooking, but it is never finished without them.

We all bring a unique taste to the pot in church and the world. The scripture says we are the salt of the earth (See Matthew 5:13-16), and though sometimes we may give off an odor and burn each other's eyes, we are all needed to complete the taste in the pot. Do not try to be what you are not called to be; each has his/her place and taste.

Day 100
Do Not Withhold Worship

I want to let you into my place of worship and its effects on me—also, my fear of wanting to worship. Worship is a verb, and we know that verbs are action words. It is not just an act where we lift our hands in corporate gatherings or at our individual meeting place of devotion. Worship must be a lifestyle for every believer. Whatever we say or do must bring honor to Jesus and show our gratitude to Him for His unfailing love and mercies.

John 4:24
God is spirit, and his worshipers must worship in the Spirit and in truth.

I misunderstood this text for so long that it drove fear into me, and I was not giving God true worship. I thought it was only because of how true and right I was that I could worship Him. I used to think that if I did not commit any sins, then I was worshipping in Spirit and truth. For a long time in my walk with God, I refused to give God worship because I thought I had done something wrong, so when I went to church, I would keep quiet, not wanting the wrath of God to fall on me.

Thank God for the knowledge of His Word, the impartation of His Spirit, and the teachings that opened my understanding so

I could learn His ways and what He requires of me. Now I worship God because of who He is and not because I think I have a right-standing with Him. We are made in right-standing with God by faith, not by what we do and do not do. I worship God because of His unmerited favour (grace). I worship God because He does not deal with me as my sins deserve. I worship God because of how merciful He has been towards me and how kind He is to allow me to come boldly before Him for forgiveness.

For me, Worshipping God has become my lifestyle, so even when I fall short, I do not withhold His worship, but I humbly acknowledge where I have fallen short and show my gratitude by correcting the error.

Do not withhold worship from God because you think you have done things you should not have done. Acknowledge your shortcomings and pick up where you left off. Now that you know, go and do accordingly.

Day 101
Brokenness Is A Part Of Your Growth

It is not very often that transparency and the acknowledgment of failures, trials, and errors are documented or talked about with the wider public. Often, a facade is put on, and it does not reflect the actual reality of our walk with Christ.

I feel what you feel, and go through similar situations as you do. My ability to document and make known my struggles and accomplishments is not saying I have it all under control, but this is a means of helping someone and learning as I go along on this Christian journey. I am not alone, and neither are you. God promised in His Word that when we go through the fire, it will not burn us, neither will the flame scorch us; the floodwaters will not overflow us, for He is with us (See Isaiah 43:2). I questioned this and sought clarification. I was told that it is so. We may feel the heat of the fire, but we will not be destroyed; in the same way, we feel the sun's heat, but it does not actually burn us.

I am not running a race to win, but I am running a race to finish. I may meet up on hurdles and find it difficult to go over. In my attempt to get over it, I may fall and sustain some injuries, but I will get up and dress my wounds. I may not go at the pace that others want, but at a pace where God can have His perfect will in my life.

Sometimes the will of God is not my will, and I stubbornly ignore, walk away and do my own thing, only to find myself back to where He had instructed me to walk. Then it seems longer and harder, but that is because I disobeyed His instructions in the first place. Yet, He is with me in my ups and downs.

I struggle to love and forgive. I struggle with the motive of rendering evil for evil. I struggle to stay in the Word of God and to apply it daily. I also struggle with the intent to act without a care because it is my life. But I am reminded that it is what comes out of my mouth that defiles me (See Matthew 15:11). I have been defiled many times, but His grace is sufficient to keep me, and His strength is made perfect in my weakness.

Your shortcomings are not a turn off for Jesus; He takes pleasure in the restoration of broken pottery.

~ Kefira Reid

Day 102
Remove The Mask

The way I portray myself will either break me or shape me. In contemplating this Christian pathway, it puts me in a state of introspection. I endeavor to be authentic and not live by my own ideas and understanding, but the challenge is to quiet the noise in and around me so I can hear the voice of God as He speaks to me.

Sometimes, it can be hard to really hear His voice as the other sounds around me are so loud, busy, and convincing that I sometimes tend to go with the loudest and most enticing sound that satisfies my ego. I do not ever want the world to think that living for Jesus is unattainable by my walk and conduct. I do not want to wear a mask so much that the mask I wear eventually becomes who I am: my true identity. 2 Corinthians 4:2 tells us: *"Rather, we have renounced secret and shameful ways; we do not use deception, nor do we distort the word of God. On the contrary, by setting forth the truth plainly we commend ourselves to everyone's conscience in the sight of God."*

This pathway is trial and error, and while I have the Manual to life (the Bible), it is not a blueprint of how to avoid the different unpleasant circumstances that will come upon me because I cannot avoid such circumstances. It is clearly outlined that I will be persecuted, wrongly accused, and even killed.

Sometimes I act as if the circumstance comes upon me suddenly, and I was not made aware of them. I go out of character many times, but it is not that I am fake. I have learned that one cannot pretend for long.

Jesus faced the same temptations we do, yet He was authentic in His life here on earth. He set an example that I should follow. Do I always follow Him? No, but I am working on them. I cannot stop anyone from thinking and behaving unpleasantly towards me, but I can put things in place to control my responses in regard to their actions.

Do not allow the decorated and enticing negative voice of reasoning to consume you so much that what you do is no longer a mask but an actual featured identity.

His blood has transformed you, and you do not have to pretend anymore. Do not dress yourself up for Him; let Him see the bare you so He can dress you Himself.

Day 103
Brush Off And Start Again

I wrote about the beating and the knockdowns that the adversary, the devil, had been giving me, not knowing how many rounds I had left. Shortly after, I ended up in the ring again. It was so subtle; I am still turning it over in my head. That is why Paul wrote in Ephesians 6:11: *"Put on the full armor of God, so that you can take your stand against the devil's schemes."* This was a hard one, and I thought I was going to get the count to ten and declared out. But GOD! These blows pierce to the soul, leaving wounds so deep, if I am not careful, I relapse into the old me and press play.

Every time I feel the urge to act a certain way, I hear those waiting for me to fall begin to rejoice and agree in great satisfaction that their expectations had become a reality. I struggle with the thought of giving in and just doing what makes me satisfied. The pressure to always portray a certain way that is totally not me does more harm than good. Whereas I am trying not to mess up, I end up not being my true self, which results in me messing up just the same.

As a Christian, I walk differently from the world; I talk differently and act differently. I know when I have strayed from the way the Lord requires. I am in no way trying to please man, and, at times, I get blinded by the very body of people to whom I am joined and how they are unified in an effort to criticize if I act differently from what they think is the right way. With every blow I get, it is the devil's expectation to get me out. I am weakened but not dead. I am wounded but not defeated. I am cast down, but not utterly destroyed.

The devil, at no time, is trying to soil or mess up an already messed up person; he goes for the pure. The devil targets us because we have been made pure through the blood of Jesus Christ. The moment we are soiled and infected, everyone will see. When that happens, we begin to think we are defective, and the old self has resurfaced. This is my advice: brush them off.

Feeling soiled? Brush them off. Do you feel the need to relapse, and do you? Hang in there; do not give in under pressure. Are you caught between indecision? Maybe you cannot see which option is better. Do not say yes, or they get their heart's desire; continue to disappoint them. You are not alone, and giving up is not a better option. You are worthy of another chance, not by man's decision, but by God's unmerited favour. You may have already soiled the garment, but His blood is a stain remover.

Day 104
Knocked Down, But Not Out

With every beating and knockout punches that I encountered, the adversary, the devil, thought I was out, but what actually happened is that while he knocked me down and thought it was over, I was brought low so I could see God in His glory, high and lifted up. When I was up and well, I relied on my own strength and capabilities; everything was done from my so-called righteousness. God clearly stated in His Word that our righteousness are like filthy rags (See Isaiah 64:6). Filthy, because we think we become right with God by what we do that others deem impressive.

When I am down low, I have no choice but to call on the name of Jesus. Fighting back with carnality will only make things worse and drives me farther away from the perfected will of God. Fighting in the flesh will only allow me to lose the battle. My lowly position is an indication of my helplessness and inabilities to maintain a continued upward composure without God being my balance. I may have to stay down for a while for the process of restoration to be complete, but when I rise, I will arise with the newness of life and the God-given strength to carry on.

I do not know how many rounds I have left to go. The thought of quitting may resurface; the persuasion to act out of hurt and on impulse may arise, but I certainly cannot do it on my own.

I may not be able to pray while I am down because I am holding on to what caused me to be down and looking at the different ways I could have handled it. I will still not be able to do any healing on my own, but I trust that God will keep me through the process. He promised never to leave me, so even when I am unfaithful, He remains faithful and true.

Have you been knocked low? You are not out.

Proverbs 24:16
For though the righteous fall seven times, they rise again, but the wicked stumble when calamity strikes.

Take the beating, squeezing and shaking; your greater will be better than your last.

Day 105
God Will Not Allow You To Fail

I could never understand the keen attention others give to the failure of another individual. For as long as I can remember, I have been a listed person for failure. Some people set their radars for the latest mishaps to take place so they can rejoice or say, "I told you so." I experienced this at school, church, in family, and in ministry. "She is not bright enough," they say. "She'll never make it."

I had to repeat the tenth grade due to circumstances beyond my control, but God came through for me. Even though I did not attend graduation, I still came out with the required number of subjects to make the graduation list.

I was not the most loved in church as I was deemed the girl with too much attitude. I was bound to create an uncomfortable scene. Even so, God disappointed them again by keeping me from backsliding and continued to perform His mastery work in making me a vessel of honor. Psalm 121 has been a theme for me as I struggled through life. Psalm 121:3 assures me that: *"He will not let your foot slip—he who watches over you will not slumber."*

When it comes to having a family, I was not the best choice for my husband, so degrading and unwelcoming remarks were

222

being thrown around: "He's poised for ministry," they said. "Her attitude is not in alignment to what a minister's wife should be." "She ago mash up him ministry." "She does not have the intellectual capacity. He needs a wife with a notable profession." God did it again because what they could not see was the Potter behind the wheel, breaking, molding, and making me into the beautiful pottery I am today. I have celebrated thirteen years of marital union at the writing of this book, and produced three beautiful children. God is good. He demonstrated His Word in me from Psalm 84:11: *"For the Lord God is a sun and shield; the Lord bestows favor and honor; no good thing does he withhold from those whose walk is blameless."*

In ministry, they hoped to hear of my failure; they were always looking for the dirt that the Lord skimmed from the top of the pot so they could rejoice. They always seemed to have a look of disappointment that I did not meet their expectations. God has kept me as I endeavored to walk in His Word.

1 Peter 3:16
Keeping a clear conscience, so that those who speak maliciously against your good behavior in Christ may be ashamed of their slander.

It has been nine years in ministry, and God has been good. He kept me from the naysayers and closed the mouths of those who continue to live in the expectancy to see me slip up.

Deuteronomy 28:13
The Lord will make you the head, not the tail. If you pay
attention to the commands of the Lord your God that I give you
this day and carefully follow them, you will always be at the
top, never at the bottom.

I am not my own; I belong to Jesus. The Lord has perfected that which concerns me. The task is mine to let you know that God can turn things around; your messy, unwelcoming, twisted life, as they consider it, is not who you are. He can turn it around for your good. He will turn it around for your good, so as they continue to wait in great anticipation with their popcorns, the salt from the butter will burn their lips as they wait for the next episode that will never be aired because God turned it around.

Day 106
Part Ways With Your Demons

I always wondered why I got the same results, regardless of the circumstances I found myself in, but then I realized that I used the same mindset to resolve my issues; hence, the results are always the same. The freedom of truth from the Holy Spirit got a hold of me, so now I know that I must defeat the things that haunt me (demons), then I must part ways with them. I must defeat and part ways with unforgiveness, bitterness, grudge, self-centeredness, and fear.

All I needed to do was make a step, and then my feet started cooperating. It felt good. I will not say I have them under control altogether because sometimes I find myself in a previous situation that I had been in before. God said in 1 Corinthians 10:13: *"No temptation has overtaken you except what is common to mankind. And God is faithful; he will not let you be tempted beyond what you can bear. But when you are tempted, he will also provide a way out so that you can endure it."*

The more we entertain these nonprofitable behaviors, the more they will be attached to us. Occasionally, because of our differences in opinions and personalities, I may offend someone, or someone offends me. Sometimes it takes time for me to come into subjection to the Holy Spirit, and I may linger in responding in the right attitude, but I have learned that if I give place to the devil, then he will occupy my being. I do not want that.

Romans 13:14
Rather, clothe yourselves with the Lord Jesus Christ, and do not think about how to gratify the desires of the flesh.

James 4:7 says: *"Submit yourselves, then, to God. Resist the devil, and he will flee from you."*

Do not miss out on the freedom to live your best life now; just lift your feet, and the movements will follow.

Day 107
Keep Your Vows To God

The Lord spoke into my spirit and said I should remember that it does not mean I should act as if I have arrived when I ask for anything, and it is granted. He says the fact that I got it, means the battle has intensified because I have to fight twice as hard to keep it. The vow I made to do and be better when I receive my request should be honored.

Sometimes we give the Lord our word to do better and manage better if He acts on our behalf, but when He does act, we start treating the very thing He blessed us with as the most important, forgetting that we gave our word to do better.

Deuteronomy 23:21-23
If you make a vow to the Lord your God, do not be slow to pay it, for the Lord your God will certainly demand it of you and you will be guilty of sin. But if you refrain from making a vow, you will not be guilty. Whatever your lips utter you must be sure to do, because you made your vow freely to the Lord your God with your own mouth.

To be the best you can be in your career takes dedication. Cut back on the leisure time others are having, and stay focused.

To keep your vow to God, you have to be dedicated and cut all distractions.

Day 108
Jesus, Our Role Model

Have you ever thought about the cost of being a role model? As I often do, I look back over my life, and I realize there is a cost for everything. There is a cost to be successful in school. There is a cost to have a successful marriage and keep it spicy. We must learn to respect, defend, and communicate with each other. Cut back on the amount of time spent with other people to facilitate spending quality time together with your spouse.

A role model is a person looked to by others as an example to be imitated. We all have someone we want to imitate, whether it is a good imitation or a bad one, not just in a spiritual sense, but holistically. As a role model, you are being watched every step of the way: the way we talk, act, and conduct ourselves generally. Those who desire to imitate us take note of how we deal with different situations that may arise. Often, we hear younger persons referring to us as role models because they see something in us to imitate.

When we imitate Jesus, we automatically take on the life of Christ, which means He becomes our role model. The path He walked is the same path we will eventually walk too.

Matthew 16:24
Then Jesus said to his disciples, "Whoever wants to be my disciple must deny themselves and take up their cross and follow me."

Jesus demonstrated what it meant to walk uprightly when He was on earth. We are not perfect beings because we were born in sin (See Psalm 51:5), but we have the freedom to go boldly before Him and ask Him to correct our wrongs and walk in His corrections. The cost to follow Jesus is high, but we will be greatly rewarded if we follow through.

Matthew 19:29
And everyone who has left houses or brothers or sisters or father or mother or wife or children or fields for my sake will receive a hundred times as much and will inherit eternal life.

Day 109
Circumstances Will Make Opportunities For You

I marvel at the awesomeness of God and the wonders He performs. God is infinite, and He can use any method He chooses to prove Himself strong and help push people into their destiny.

Let us consider Pharaoh, Moses, and the children of Israel. God could have done things differently. He could have easily delivered them, but He used Pharaoh to prove to His people how awesome He is. Moses ran away after killing the Egyptian and lived in the wilderness for forty years. God was preparing him for something bigger and greater than he could imagine, and his experience would be needed to bring the children out of Egypt. This is how God works.

As much as I complain and hurt when I am plunged into difficult moments in life and situations that cause me to agonize and hurt, God uses all the misunderstandings, ill-treatments, and other variables that came about—whether by my own doing or from people—to give me a better tomorrow. As much as they irritate me, I love people because without them and the unpleasant circumstances, my page "Expensive Experiences" would not have been realized.

Day 110
Be Careful Of Your Associations

If you associate with liars, you eventually become a liar. If you associate with a hater, you will become hateful. If you hang around people who gossip, you will eventually be a gossiper. If you are around people who pray, you will become a prayer warrior. If you are around people who encourages, you become an encourager. If you hang out with people who serve, you become a servant leader.

We must avoid bitter and unforgiving people, never transforming, or who cause discord among the brethren. You will become like the company that you keep.

Corinthians 15:33
Do not be misled: "Bad company corrupts good character."

#imnotperfectiamReal

Day 111
Forgiveness Matters

When you are adamant about repaying evil for evil, you know you have fallen from grace. Be careful how you allow the devil to manipulate and rob you of the joy and blessings of knowing God. Allow the continued fellowship between the Trinity and you to be alive.

When I speak blessings, I am not talking about the physical because not all material things are blessings. Sometimes, material possessions are trouble wrapped up in disguise. I am talking about the relationship between you and God. Even if you stumble, you can still be called His friend because you are blameless, meaning there are no secrets between you and God. If you want the relationship to remain open and free, forgive quickly. If we want to be forgiven, we must forgive.

We sometimes get so caught up with being spiritual, and after the rush and excitement at church, we cannot live out what we gained from our experiences. So, our church life and everyday life are conflicting with the truth of living a Christian life. Thank God He is a God of a second chance. He gave Nineveh a second chance, and He is giving us the same option: we can choose to live in our rebellion or make a change.

Self-examination, how about you?

Day 112
Being Grateful In Everything

Have you ever wondered why you are still alive when there are so many faithful and saved persons passing on? You know you are not even deserving of the gift of life from God. I wonder about this sometimes, and I know it is not because of anything good that I have done.

I am a sinner saved by grace, and His grace continuously carries me. His grace and mercy have become my life-support machine, and I am so grateful He has not pulled the plug because sometimes I am just so unresponsive. The moment I realize that my eyes are open, and I am not in a holding place of death, I become so overjoyed and grateful. I go on with each day that I am alive with thankfulness because He did not have to do it, but He did.

The things that overwhelm me become dim because His mercies are renewed to me. I am not a showoff; I am a product of gratefulness.

Being thankful makes room for increase.
~ Kefira Reid

Day 113
A Conversation With Jesus Changes Things

While sitting and thinking one day, a sudden depression came over me. Maybe you have had this experience as well where you are all good, but then a sudden weird feeling overshadows you. Yes, I had one of those moments. I immediately started talking to God, and He was talking back.

Thank God I serve a God who responds. He said, "It's not the ritualistic things you do that puts you in a relationship with Me; it's the relationship we have that causes you to do those rituals, like reading the Word and praying, which is basically having a conversation."

When you are in a relationship with someone, communication is key. It allows you to get to know the person better: their likes, dislikes, what makes them happy and what makes them sad.

You pay attention to what is said and done in a relationship. Likewise, being in a relationship with Jesus means you study His Word so you get to know Him because His physical presence is not here. You study to know what He likes, dislikes, and what makes Him happy, so you learn to do as He does.

Galatians 1:10
Am I now trying to win the approval of human beings, or of God? Or am I trying to please people? If I were still trying to please people, I would not be a servant of Christ.

When we know what Jesus likes, we will aim to please Him. When you are in a functional and loving relationship, every time something happens, the first person you want to share it with is him or her. Every time I experience disappointment, joy, something good or bad, the first person I talk to is Jesus. He lets me know we are in a relationship, so that is okay. You will not confide in a stranger; you always tell your problems to a friend.

So, let me encourage you if you are experiencing a bout of depression: feelings will come, but if you are in a relationship with Jesus, tell Him how you are feeling and start the conversation rolling. He will respond. I can assure you; you will feel better. Completely better.

Conclusion

In writing this book, I learned that the Bible is relevant for the 21st century, as it was in times past. The experiences we face today are not new to anyone. We can all live the spoken word, and we can live it in its fullness. We face many trials because we are Christians, and we represent Jesus Christ. Just like Jesus, many well-spoken of prophets and apostles lived life in a practical way. We have their examples to follow.

Most importantly, what I discovered while writing this book is that I am never alone, even when it seems like I am. The experiences I have are not unique to me only, but my response to any given situation is an experience that can be shared with someone who may be going through the same and need encouragement.

About the Author

Kefira Reid is a born-again Christian who loves the Lord dearly and is committed to serving Him with her whole heart, body, and soul. She is a wife and mother of three beautiful children: two boys and a girl. She started serving the Lord at the age of twelve and celebrated twenty-five years of walking with the Lord in April 2020. Over two decades of walking with the Lord was not without its challenges, both in marriage ministry and her personal life. Her persistence to live the called life is what plunged her into these experiences.

Everyone has a story to tell, and the best way to tell these stories is through practical experiences. Kefira Reid will help you on your Christian journey and give you Biblical and practical experiences and encouragement to help you finish this Christian journey in a practical and fulfilling way, loving Jesus to the end.

www.ingramcontent.com/pod-product-compliance
Lightning Source LLC
LaVergne TN
LVHW051228080426
835513LV00016B/1472